Out Of The Dark Triangle

Penetrating the spiritual darkness of Indonesia—a Papuan role model in ministry.

*By
David L. Scovill based on the oral narrative in
Indonesian by Karlos Buburayai*

Copyright © 2012 by David L. Scovill

Out of the Dark Triangle
by David L. Scovill based on the oral narrative in Indonesian by Karlos Buburayai

Printed in the United States of America

ISBN 9781624191251

All rights reserved solely by the author. The author guarantees all contents are original and do not infringe upon the legal rights of any other person or work. No part of this book may be reproduced in any form without the permission of the author. The views expressed in this book are not necessarily those of the publisher.

Unless otherwise indicated, Bible quotations are taken from the New International Version of the Bible. Copyright © 1978 by the New York International Bible Society.

www.xulonpress.com

Dedicated to:

- The many young men and women whose love for Christ and passion to serve takes them into the spiritually dark enclaves of this world with the Light of the Gospel.

- The Yulius Hikinda family who played a major role in the discipling and in the mentoring of this young man into the ministry.

- Our many friends who have faithfully prayed for and sacrificially given to our ministry of mentoring men and women like Karlos into ministry in Indonesia for over half a century.

- The Indonesian believers and businessmen whose lives have been touched by Karlos' life and ministry and who give generously to bring reality to his ministry dreams.

- The peoples of The Dark Triangle whose lives have been transformed by the Gospel of Jesus Christ and among whom the Church has taken root.

Table of Contents

Part 1: The Prologue........................ 15

Chapter 1:   God's Instrument: An Earthquake.... 17
Chapter 2:   God's Angel — a Grubby Little Man .. 24
             Map of The Dark Triangle.......... 27
Chapter 3:   The Voice from Beneath the Soil 32

**Part 2: The Birth, the Boyhood, and the
         Bondage of a Lad Called "Kairo" 39**

Chapter 4:   "Kairo" ......is Born 41
Chapter 5:   Nature Produces Questions 46
Chapter 6:   Nature, My Teacher, Points me to the
             Creator.......................... 53
Chapter 7:   A Visit from One in a White Robe ... 58
Chapter 8:   Opposition Began: "Worms will Feed
             on your Dead Body!" 69
Chapter 9:   Opposition Intensified: Another Visit
             from the White-Robed One......... 75
Chapter 10: More Doubts, Another Visit: Call
             Confirmed 80

vii

Part 3: Formal and Informal Preparation for Ministry 85

Chapter 11: Head and Heart Preparation Continues 87
Chapter 12: Relief from Those Hunting Dogs 94
Chapter 13: Death Keeps Stalking Me 99
Chapter 14: A Power Encounter at Sea 104
Chapter 15: Worshipping in Our Mother Tongue . 108
Chapter 16: Challenge to Become Self-Sufficient 111

Part 4: Seminary and Commencement of Ministry 113

Chapter 17: The Whisper was Clear: Lampung, Lampung 115
Chapter 18: To Lampung and Return with My Rp. 20,000 Intact 121
Chapter 19: Ministry: Kedondong 125
Chapter 20: Ministry: Karang Sari 130

Part 5: Marriage, Mercy and More Ministry ... 139

Chapter 21: A Broken Marriage and a Bankrupt Ministry...Almost! 141
Chapter 22: Our Ministry is Being Monitored ... 151
Chapter 23: Burned Out 157
Chapter 24: That "Crazy Evangelist!" 165
Chapter 25: A Jihadist Becomes a Pastor 176
Chapter 26: The Word Spread: Bukit Kemuning and Beyond 183

Table of Contents

Chapter 27: And the Word Continued to Spread . 192
Chapter 28: Christmas ...in the Citra Village 200
Chapter 29: Experiencing "God Things"
in Ministry.................... 203

Part 6: A Special Message to My Muslim Friends......................... 209

An Explanation........................... 211
An Invitation............................. 219

An Introduction

My wife and I have spent more than fifty years in church-planting ministries in three geographical areas of the Republic of Indonesia: among the Western Dani tribe in the heart of Papua, Indonesia; among the peoples of the Waropen area; and in the Greater Indonesia—Jakarta, the capital city of Indonesia and the island of Sumatera.

Emerging from our church-planting focus among the different ethnic groups of these areas are the people—individuals, in whom we have poured our lives. You can read the incredible story of the Western Dani tribe's conversion to Christ in my book, "**The Amazing Dani**." You will be blessed and challenged!

The second geographical area upon which we focused in the latter part of the 1970s and the 1980s is called the Waropen area—a vast, undeveloped jungle area on the northwestern hip of this great island of Papua, formerly known as Irian Jaya. This is the area which, in missionary jargon, we have identified as The Dark Triangle. (See map on page 27).

Little did we know that from The Dark Triangle would come a man who would feel the call of God upon his life not only to minister to his own people in The Dark Triangle, but to move across the western part of the Indonesian archipelago bringing the Light of the Gospel to the Muslims, Buddhists and Hindus on the island of Sumatera. And that is the story of this book.

David Livingston to Africa, David Brainard to the American Indians, Hudson Taylor to China, C.T. Studd to India—all were our role models in ministry and extremely influential in assisting us in our journey "to the nations."

But we also need Papuan men and women whom God has chosen and equipped to be role models in ministry to the growing church in Papua. This story of Karlos is meant to be just that! The call of God upon his life, his love for the Lord, his understanding of Scripture and his passion to witness and to bring others to Christ whenever and wherever will thrill your heart as you read this autobiography. This is Karlos' story as told to me.

As you will note, since we are part of his story, I have written the Prologue to allow you to see how it all began. And in a unique way, this story of Karlos is also your story, for we are indebted to you who have given to, and prayed for, our ministry for over half a century. Without your sacrifices, we would have no story to tell.

Karlos' God is a big God; his faith is an active faith based on the Word of God; his spiritual gifts of

An Introduction

evangelism and spiritual discernment are evident to all.

Perhaps his story will raise some eyebrows: the power of spiritual darkness and demons which he confronted; the visits and encouragement he received from the white-robed One; the healings in answer to prayer in the name of Jesus; his discernment regarding the spirit world out of which he came—all are the natural, non-theatrical flow of living the Christian life among the peoples to whom he ministers.

Thank you for the role you have played in our lives in helping us prepare men like Karlos to continue what we began.

Though the mission organization under which we have served since 1959 has changed its name to Crossworld, since the former name, UFM International, is better known to our supporting and reading constituency, that is the name which we have used in this story.

An expression of our thanks belongs to Mrs. Grace Davies who, once again, has turned her experienced literary eye on this manuscript making it more readable.

Part 1

The Prologue

Chapter 1

God's Instrument: An Earthquake

The night was dark and the weather was chilly as I went to bed that night in the highlands of Papua, Indonesia, at one of our mission airstrips called Okbap. Weary, I lay down on the small army cot which the UFM family, the Stanzsus, had prepared for me in their home. And since we had no electricity, very methodically I put my flashlight within reach at the side of my cot—sometimes we hunted rats at night—pulled the covers over me, and sank into a restful sleep.

Several hours later, in my sleep I heard the deafening sound of a huge locomotive rushing towards me. Then, it was on me. Awakening out of my sleep, I tried to scream as my cot was tossed from side to side. "Aha, an earthquake. I've gotta get out of here," I realized as my cot heaved then collapsed under me. I reached out to grab my flashlight left standing there by my bedside.

But as I reached for it in the darkness, the earth convulsed again and my hand hit the flashlight, sending it careening somewhere towards the far side of the room. "Forget that. Just get out of here," my brain screamed, "But where is the door to get out of this bedroom?" I staggered about the room searching for it as the entire house creaked and groaned, giving every indication it would implode around me.

In the frightening darkness, my hands groped along the wooden wall paneling. There had to be a window, a door, an opening to get out before the house self-destructed. There it was—a window. But where was the door? Whose house was I in? My sleepy stupor suddenly cleared. In a flash it all came back.

In my role as the field chairman of the Unevangelized Fields Mission (UFM) in Papua, I was on one of my quarterly field visits overnighting with the Gerd and Maria Stanszus family. Still half asleep and with the room rocking and rolling about me, I ran my hand along the wall paneling and touched a door frame. "Here it is!" I swung open the door and dashed through it only to bang into the inside closet wall. But it woke me fully and I realized, "This is the closet door; the bedroom door is over here." And I stumbled toward it.

Outside I heard a voice shouting above the crashing of trees and huge boulders above us. "God save us; God spare us. What shall we do? Where shall we go? God, my family—save them!" Now fully awake, I sprang for the outside door from where I had heard Gerd calling for divine help. With the family who by that time were all outside, we stood with arms about one another, crying to

God for mercy and deliverance while the ground under us heaved and cleaved, and while boulders half the size of the house came crashing down the mountainside above us. Where could we go? Where could we flee for safety?

Then I heard it again—from far across the valley—the sound of an oncoming locomotive. As it approached, my immediate impulse was to run, to get out of its way, for it was heading straight for us. But my mind screamed, "It can't be a train. We are in the mountains of Papua where there are not even roads."

By now the sound was deafening. I braced myself for the hit, and it came. The ground heaved violently under our feet then was reduced to shudders and tremors with the locomotive sound moving past us into the distance. And we were left, crying in fear but praising the Lord because we, with the Stanszus family, had been spared. Even the house was left on its foundational posts.

The tremors and the locomotive sounds continued through that night and several nights afterward. For safety reasons, we had located under a large tarp in sleeping bags and blankets—many of the local tribespeople with us—on a little knoll a short distance away from the house, where the crashing boulders could not reach us.

The following morning, we switched on our Single Side Band radio to receive reports of the damage on other of our airstrips and houses in that vast area. One of the first reports we heard was from a Mission Aviation

Fellowship (MAF) pilot intentionally flying over the devastation. We were stunned when he remarked on the plane radio, "Folks, I can't believe it. I can't believe it! This place looks like the desert of Arizona."

Mountains had collapsed into the rivers and valleys below. River channels had been re-formed. Cavernous scars had reshaped the beautiful majestic mountains now stripped of its lush green coverage of trees and brush, simple villages with their round grass-roofed houses built on terraced hillsides and sweet potato gardens dotting the landscape were destroyed. All had become a scarred barren wasteland as far as the eye could see. The mountains were bare; the rivers were plugged with debris.

Incredible landslides had closed off rivers, with huge lakes forming behind them. These lakes eventually broke, sending millions of gallons of water cascading down those steep valleys, denuding the valleys of any lower vegetation, changing the course of the rivers and dumping the debris of trees, rocks, native houses and a few bodies literally miles out into the lowlands.

After the tremors subsided, the work of rebuilding began. Missionary houses had to be jacked back onto their posts, airstrips had to be repaired, gardens of the nationals had to be replanted wherever land could be found. Thousands were without food and shelter for days. Sickness was prevalent throughout the area with many dying from the common cold.

God's Instrument: An Earthquake

Aid poured in—from governments as well as private organizations. I smile when I remember one smartly dressed gentleman representing USAID who had just climbed off the plane at Sentani having arrived from Jakarta.

`Upon learning that I was the head of the mission working in the earthquake area and gathering relief supplies for MAF to fly them into the area, he pushed his way through the crowd at the small Sentani airport and handed me a check for ten thousand dollars, saying, "Forget the formalities and the photos. This will help begin the relief and rehabilitation of the area. There will be more from where this has come."

Several months later, with houses rebuilt and gardens again producing food for the local population, I was called to speak with the head of the Department of Health services in Jayapura.

"Mr. Scovill," he began. "Do not be anxious that I have asked you to come. Over the years, we have observed the work of missions in Papua and more recently the relief and rehabilitation of those in the earthquake area. We know that pioneering in the mountainous areas of Papua is very difficult and costly.

We have no airplanes, or trained carpenters who can tough it out and walk out with the job done. Yet you missions are doing it with amazing success and incredible quality. Would you consider helping us build five simple clinics throughout that earthquake area to give health assistance to that suffering people? We will produce the finances to do whatever you need to do." And he paused and waited my answer.

He was right. We had built several small airstrips throughout the area. We had established good working relationships with and had the confidences of the people there. We had trained and trusted simple carpenters from Daniland who had helped build the buildings at those airstrip sites.

I nodded my tentative approval, then asked, "What do you need from us to move ahead?" His reply was immediate, "All I need is a sketch of a simple building with budget figures for us to approve, and the finances will be transferred to you."

After giving careful thought to all the possible costs involved, including a possible error figure of 30 percent, I brought this to him. He looked at my building sketch and nodded his approval, then looked at my budget figures and chuckled—shaking his head. "In no way can you put those buildings up for that price. I'm going to double those figures." Which he did, and transferred the funds. He had chuckled because an estimate from any of his local coastal cronies would have been three to four times that amount with multiple headaches for him.

I had one more question needing clarification. "Sir," I asked. "What do you want done with any excess?"

He was too stunned to speak. This had never been

asked in any of his bargaining deals. "It is yours to use as your mission desires," he responded. Then he stood indicating that the deal was approved, the funds would be transferred, and when finished he would visit each site to see that all was well. He did and we did—with great results in the building and development of those communities AND with a balance of several thousand dollars.

Those funds allowed our mission to pioneer into a new area we eventually called The Dark Triangle, for which we had been praying and pondering a mission strategy for several years. Lacking funds, we had not been able to move. With those funds we could, and we did.

This is the beginning of my story of God's divine hand upon a young man coming out of The Dark Triangle and his subsequent ministry throughout Indonesia.

Chapter 2

God's Angel—A Grubby Little Man!

Though the passing of years has dimmed my memory of the precise detail, on one of my visits to the government offices regarding the rehabilitation and development in that earthquake area, while waiting for my appointment with the head of the Department of Health I was approached by a man whom I had never met.

His clothes were grubby; his unwashed body odor was offensive and his manner strange. I turned my head away from him knowing that I would soon be called to speak with the Department of Health official. It did not work.

He approached me with a big smile which covered his face, exposing teeth layered with the dark red stain of the betel nut he had been chewing and spitting for years. He was chewing such a mouthful when he approached, but in order to speak with me, he turned and spit his wad into a nook near the stairs, then extended his hand of greeting, introducing himself.

God's Angel—A Grubby Little Man!

He was Bernardos Imbiri, the People's Representative for the Barapasi district of the Upper Waropen regional area on the northwestern hip of the island. He was currently in Jayapura seeking government help for the incredibly needy and forgotten people of his area. He was still speaking when my call came, so I excused myself and went into the office. I did not need to hear any more hopeless, desperate pleas for peoples needing our mission's help and I secretly hoped this to be the end of our friendly conversation.

It was not. An hour later when I came out of the office, he was still waiting for me. It was more than a courtesy. For some unknown reason, suddenly I was overcome with the strange feeling that I should hear him out. Was this not the area that our mission (UFM) had targeted for its next advance? Was this a Divine Hand bringing us together? We sat down on the dirty steps of those cement stairs and I listened.

He was passionate as he spoke of the needs of his people congregated in small villages along the large rivers of that vast area. The people lived off the fish in the rivers and the wild boars and birds of the jungle. Malaria, leprosy, elephantiasis and addiction to their local homemade liquor was destroying his people. Their youth were uneducated. The leadership of the traditional Dutch Reformed Church in most of the areas depended on a sip or two of their homemade whiskey to produce a Bible Story with comments on Sunday, and the government personnel was corrupt and frequently involved in drunken village brawls.

He leaned toward me, tears forming in his eyes, and grasped my hand, pleading passionately, "Cannot your mission help us? We know what missions has done for the peoples of the interior. Why have we on the coast been left to self-destruct in utter hopelessness? Does no one care for us?" That was all I needed to begin to propel my thinking and our mission, UFM International, into the Upper Waropen regional area, and to the home village of Mr. Imbiri who would help us pioneer into what later became known in missionary jargon as The Dark Triangle.

The Dark Triangle is a geographical area within three locations on the map which, when one connects those three points with straight lines, forms a huge triangular land mass which our mission identifies as The Dark Triangle. (See sketch on next page.)

We called it The Dark Triangle because of the difficulty of getting into the area, the disease and degradation of the people, and the domination of evil spirits and the fear which regulated their lives. This area was populated by a people moving into what anthropology calls Cultural Disequilibrium, in which cultures destroy themselves with their people.

God's Angel—A Grubby Little Man!

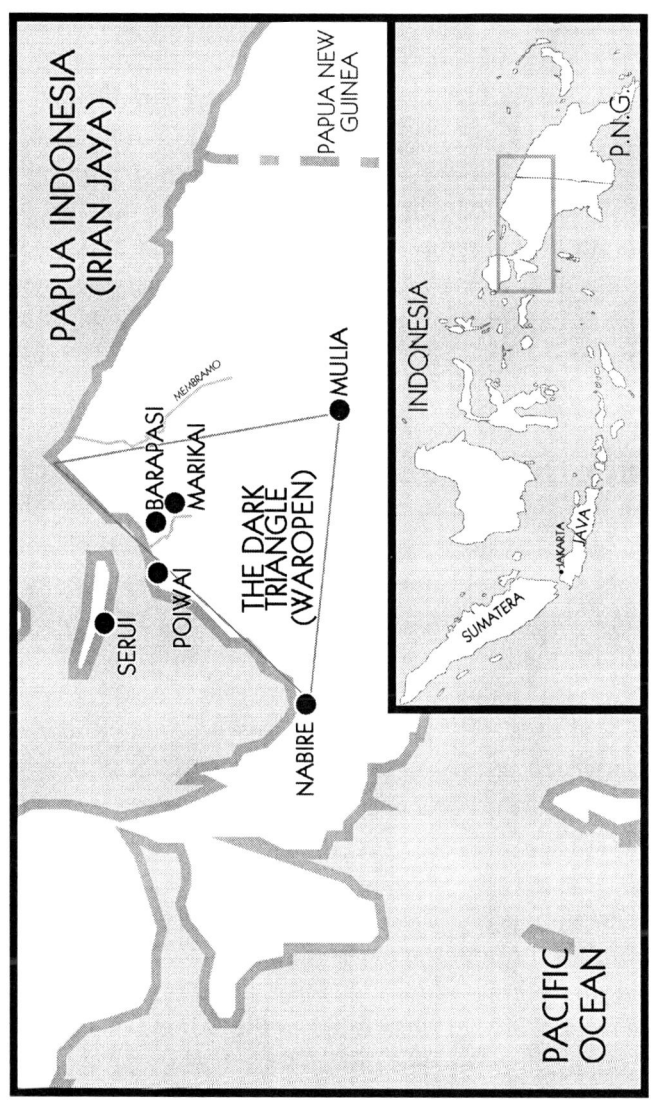

Months after my conversation with Mr. Imbiri in the Department of Health, when weather and winds permitted, we landed in the MAF helicopter in the middle of the soccer field at the government post called Barapasi, the village of Mr. Imbiri. With no prior communication, we wondered if we would see our little friend again. We were not long in waiting. For up the muddy path through the unkempt village came a shout and a small grubby man in ragged shirt and shorts, chewing a wad of betel nut, pushed his way through the crowd to welcome us.

Pastor Bert Koirewoa, the head of our national church, The Evangelical Church of Indonesia, had come with us. This church numbering over 100,000 members was born and grew exponentially during the 1960s and 1970s when thousands of tribes-people from the mountainous highland areas of the interior of Papua rejected their animistic way of life and became fellow believers in Christ. Pastor Bert was from the Lower Waropen regional area. His village was located on another large river which fed into the ocean down the coastline several hours travel in a dug-out canoe powered by a small outboard motor.

Preliminaries cared for and the purpose of our visit identified through the assistance of Mr. Imbiri, we were grudgingly granted permission to hold several evenings of evangelistic services there in the village of Barapasi. In preparation for that time with whoever might come, we bathed in the river and dressed for the evening service. We knew we were in hostile territory; word of our coming representing an active and fast growing church other than the traditional dead Dutch Reformed Church had preceded us.

Nevertheless, we were visitors and an attraction. Most of the villagers attended, along with the government officials of the area who were sitting in the honored seats at the front. It was obvious they had "sipped" of their local homemade liquor before entering the building.

These buildings were built with only half-walls and of local materials to catch whatever breeze might be blowing in that suffocating heat. Since the local liquor made from the sago trees along the river was the main reason for the village brawls, lethargy and degradation of the people, Bert bravely began his devotional on The Curse of Alcohol.

Passionate was he in delivering his message, and the more passionately he preached, the louder the commotion and raucous drunken laughter of the government personnel and elders of the Dutch Reformed Church group up on the front bench. Unable to quiet the preacher, they turned up the volume level of the tape cassette recorder they were using to a loud squeal.

This was too much for me. I rose quietly, walked to the front as inconspicuously as possible, reached down and pulled the microphone jack out of their tape recorder, wrapped it in its cord, stuck it in my pocket and went back to my seat. The squealing ceased, the crowd smiled, and the message continued. Even the drunken government personnel and church elders up front fell silent, some of them sleeping and others listening.

Following the service, I gave the microphone back to the leading government officer saying, "Of all people who need to embrace the message Pastor Bert was giving, you men should be the first, by example, to lead your people who are seeking the truth and are in desperate need of a new way of life."

He mumbled an apology then left as the people crowded around us, tears in their eyes, affirming their need and desire for more of the truth which had warmed their hearts that evening. We spent several nights teaching in that village, and with Mr. Imbiri and other caring government officials, mapped out a strategy for helicopter visits to several other villages which we were asked to visit, in hopes we could begin a ministry in those areas as well.

While other government and Dutch Reformed Church officials glumly looked on, Mr. Imbiri, as the People's Representative for the area, excitedly spoke of the government's plan to move the entire village upriver to another large area which would accommodate their expansive plans for the future.

The current site was dismal and dirty, always muddy, and heavily infested with mosquitoes and consequently with malaria. Even the drinking water was contaminated by the large muddy river flowing past the village, for the villagers upstream used it for their toilets. Frequent flooding was eating away at the banks of their current village location. The government was insisting they move and we could feel their mounting excitement as they spoke.

This was a tiny window of hope for those of the older generation holding on to the possibility of a better way of life in which their children could have a proper education.. These were the men who wanted not only the material help from the government for this move, but also for the spiritual help which would come from our mission.

Chapter 3

The Voice from Beneath the Soil

It was the end of the year 1977; the name of that relocation site was the village of Marikai. This is where the story of Karlos begins.

The Upper Waropen regional area in the province of Papua Indonesia is a vast jungle area bordered by the Pacific Ocean on the north and west and gradually moves up into the northwest-southeast mountain ranges of the interior. Rivers wind their way out of those mountain ranges then laze through hundreds of miles of dense jungle, eventually terminating in the ocean on the north and west. Rains in those mountains produce swollen, turbulent rivers which often quite mercilessly change the course of the rivers, piling them and not infrequently, closing them, with trees and other debris.

In the upper regions of this vast area, nomadic tribes feed on the fish in the rivers and streams, and hunt the wild boar and cassowary birds that roam the jungle. Fighting to protect their tribe's fishing and hunting areas is frequent, but so is the stealthy, and at times violent, pursuit to kidnap young girls to take to their men. Sickness and death in childbearing make women and young girls a much needed commodity for survival in this harsh environment. If their own tribe cannot provide a mate for their young men, they look to steal her from other tribes bordering on their hunting and fishing land boundaries.

In their search for survival, they keep their houses simple and very temporary—often just a few poles tied together with easy-to-obtain vines or bark, and branches and leaves for roof and walls—to protect their privacy. This is their shelter from the rain and a place where they can cook their fish or wild boar then lie down around the fire to sleep throughout the night slapping at the hoards of mosquitoes which descend on them seeking to satisfy their thirst on their victim's blood and, at the same time, often injecting their victim's red blood cells with malaria.

The highways of that vast area are the rivers; the vehicle of transportation and survival is their dug-out canoe. In this, the family, consisting normally of a man with his wife, several small children and always a skinny hunting dog, will float downstream with the current, hastened by the tide moving back to the ocean, or hitchhike with the current of the tide moving upriver from the ocean.

In the canoe is normally a handful of red-hot coals from which they fire their tobacco, or blow them into a small fire to cook their fish, crocodile meat, and often fruit and nuts which they find along the banks of the rivers or at abandoned stopping spots along the way.

If they find a good fishing spot, or the obvious telltale signs of the run of wild boars, they will throw up a small shack of poles, branches and leaves, gather some firewood, and spend the night—or several nights—hunting, fishing, smoking and drying their meat, before they move on. The mood is leisurely, lazy, and patient with mother nature on whom they depend for their sustenance and survival in that harsh environment.

No one knows the month or the year, but into this scene comes a man with his wife and small family. A war between clans has driven them out of the foothills to seek space and good soil into a new area which promises food and safety from their enemies.

His only clothing is a small piece of bark or large leaf covering his private parts and tied with a vine about his waist. Scars on his chest indicate his prowess in the tribal wars and often the number of people he has killed; two needle-like bones from the leg of a jungle possum or cassowary bird protrude upright from the tip of his nose; his lips and teeth are red from the betel nut he has chewed and spit since he was a small boy. His eyes have that glassy, distant look from the drug of that nut.

His wife is naked but for a small piece of tree bark which dangles loosely in front of her genital area and hanging loosely around her hips is a skirt made from leaves. In a type of cloth made from tree bark beaten until supple is wrapped a crying infant; it hangs in front of her in easy reach of her breasts to nurse when needed.

They have left the mountains and have drifted downriver toward the ocean, hunting, fishing and looking for a place to settle their small family.

They don't know, nor do they care, how long it will take. All they need for survival is in the jungle around them, the water beneath them and whatever is on their simple raft made from a few poles tied together or in that dug-out canoe which the man directs along the water lanes with a long pole as he stands on the back tip of the dug-out.

Their eyes scan the jungle along the banks of the river looking for a suitable place—land for gardening, springs or clean streams for drinking, rivers and streams to supply their daily fare of fish and crabs and trees: nut trees, fruit trees, and especially the sago tree which produces the main food of their diet called *papeda*, a wet flour made from the sago tree which when heated in hot water becomes a clear glue-like paste palatable only when eaten with river greens or cooked fish.

They tie their simple raft, on which they have been carried downstream by the river currents, to a sturdy bush on a small sandy spot of beach made hospitable for the occasion by the overflow of a recent flooding. Weary from their river travel, after resting and building a fire to light his smoke the man beats back the tall grass along the river bank then, using small poles, he frames a hasty shelter where they enjoy some respite from the heat of the day and the rain of the evening.

As the darkness of night accompanied by the buzz of myriads of mosquitoes descends upon them they fall into a fitful sleep, exhausted by the day's heat and by the continual slapping at the hordes of mosquitoes seeking their blood.

Early the next morning while the wife nurses her child and roasts nuts and sago biscuits for the day's food needs, the man picks up his bow and arrows and his machete, calls to the dog, and they disappear into the jungle in search of a suitable site to build a more permanent house. He has been told that the name of the area is Marikai; he notices the telltale signs of others who have hunted in those forests or perhaps even have a small home hidden somewhere close to the river from where they can move out to fish.

As he moves through the jungle, he notices the sago trees, and the nut and fruit trees growing in abundance. The soil is loamy—very good for gardening and planting of banana trees. Then he hears a voice. At first only the sound of a whisper but it increases in intensity as he moves on toward a small stream fed my multiple underground springs.

The voice is louder now and seems to come from somewhere beneath the ground, "I am Buburayai; I am Buburayai." He knows immediately that it is the spirit of the soil inviting him to locate on the site near the springs, with promise of that spirit's protection and provision. It is here that he settles with his family and takes the family name from the voice which spoke to him from beneath the soil: Buburayai.

To them were born eight children with only five surviving the rigors of childbirth and their hostile environment. Our story concerns the sixth child of this family; he continues telling the saga of his own life and ministry.

Part 2

***The Birth
The Boyhood and
The Bondage
of a Lad Called Kairo***

Chapter 4

"Kairo" (Satan impersonating the form of a dragon) Is Born!

I was born in a small hut in the middle of the forest. In keeping with the custom of my people, it is forbidden for any male to come near the place in the forest where the women have their babies. In that special place somewhat of a distance from the village, a small area is fenced in with a simple round hut in the center which only the women can enter to have their babies and/or during their menstrual cycle.

Even the dogs, should they venture near that small round shelter, are driven away as are all other animals. Because that small fenced in area is considered unclean, anyone who ventures near is contaminated, pronounced unclean and will not be protected or blessed by the spirits worshipped in that part of the forest. It was in this small child-bearing hut that I was born, the sixth male of the family.

Each expectant mother who goes there to give birth must undergo a spirit rite in which a magic incantation is cited over her. The shaman takes a container of water, breathes into it a special portent while reciting a magic incantation. Then, this is given to the expectant mother to drink; it guarantees her protection as well as the protection of her child during its birth.

Following the birth, the umbilical cord is severed with a special bamboo knife especially sharpened for the occasion. Though there are many types of bamboo in the forest and along the rivers, this is a special bamboo split and sharpened to accomplish this procedure following which the mother must stay in that hut for one to two months until she is free of any emission and completely healed of any trauma resulting from the birth of her child.

Returning to her village and family responsibilities before she is completely free of any emission, defiles the entire village and brings defilement upon the men of that village. This robs them of their power to hunt and fish and, since the spirit is offended, of any protection or provision by that spirit. If it is felt that the woman has defiled the village, she is often killed with bow and arrow.

It was here that I was born and given the name "Kairo," the name for "Satan." My people believed that Marikai, my village, was the stronghold of Satan who controlled the area. Thus, in a conciliatory gesture and in the hopes that I would bring a greater spiritual power into the family, I was given his name "Kairo." Others were given good names; I have no idea why I was given such an horrific childhood name.

"Kairo" (Satan impersonating the form of a dragon) Is Born!

During those early years of my life, my mother would take me with her to hunt for food in the jungle and to fish in the rivers and streams. Anticipating childbirth, the mothers would make a carrying pouch from the bark of a certain tree. They would beat the tree with a crude club until the bark would loosen and could be stripped off. Then it was pounded again for several hours until the rough bark scales on the outside of the bark separated and fell away, leaving the inner more supple layer to be used to make a piece of soft material almost like a piece of cloth from which the pouch could be formed. After being dried in the sun, the mothers would tie this into a pouch in which the child was carried. It was also used to make crude coarse blankets in which the child was wrapped.

In this I was carried, slung from my mother's neck and/or shoulder and resting on her hip or against her bosom as she daily left the village to hunt for food and fish. Finding a small pool of water in the stream bed which had potential for hiding small fish or crabs, she would hang me on the branch of a nearby tree, then with her friends would either drain the small pool of water or empty it by using a small shovel-like part of the sago tree branch, after which she would pick up the fish and crabs hiding in its depths. I was hung high up on the branches out of danger from wild animals such as snakes, wild boars, and the large dragon like animal called the komodo.

As I grew older, I experienced many dangerous events in my life. While still a baby, I fell into the fire;

I was badly burned but did not die. It seems the family was not very happy with me—the young child. As a toddler 3 or 4 years old, I learned later that the people had made plans to take me deep into the jungle to be killed and eaten by wild animals of the forest, but those plans did not materialize.

Later, when I was 4 or 5 years old, we went out to hunt for food. On our return trip back to the village, while walking through the jungle I was bitten by a poisonous cobra snake. All of my brothers ran abandoning me. By the time I arrived toddling home behind them, the poison in my system had shut down my voice; I could no longer speak.

I could hear my family speaking, but their voices were slurred and indistinct. I wanted to answer them but the only noise I could make was an indistinct "gaah, gaah" gagging sound. My body burned with a fierce fever then turned cold, bluish and swollen. I had no strength or desire to live; only my beating heart gave evidence of life within me.

Fearful that I was going to die, and thinking that perhaps I was gagging on something, my mother thrust her finger into my mouth scooping out the mucous that was accumulating. My father in a fit of anger grabbed his bow and arrow to take revenge on my brothers and friends who had left me to die there in the jungle following the encounter with the snake. Looking back it seems there was still a bit of compassion in his heart for me, his son.

"Kairo" (Satan impersonating the form of a dragon) Is Born!

Sometime later, I was bitten again, and then a few months later, again. This occurred six or seven times during those early years of my life. And while others of my childhood years were bitten and died, for some reason I was spared, though at times there seemed to be no hope and breathing was difficult.

Another time I fell into a treacherous flooded river and was drowning when my older brother jumped into the water and rescued me from the strong current that was dragging me downstream to my death.

As I look back, though unaware of it at the time, I have the distinct feeling that a Divine Hand was sovereignly protecting and guiding me in the growing up process of my life because of a specific plan and a divine purpose God had for me. I was soon to realize that.

Chapter 5

Nature Produces Questions

As I continued to grow, I was able to join my elders and older brothers on their hunting excursions. My task was often carrying the arrows for the hunt. Tagging along after them, I was able to observe more intently the beauty of nature around me, especially in the jungle around Marikai. The sweet sounds of the birds singing to one another as they flitted from tree to tree accompanied us as we walked.

Of particular interest was the *nuri* bird. The further we walked the greater the possibility we would hear this bird deep in the jungle and we would stop to determine from which direction the song came. This is the bird which would direct the wild boar, the cassowary bird, or other jungle animals to us guaranteeing our hunt to be successful. The elders of our village are convinced this can occur because of their special spirit rituals inciting the *nuri* bird to locate and direct the animals toward us for our hunt.

Growing up, I thoroughly enjoyed our hunting and fishing routines. The rivers were our highways, and the

Nature Produces Questions

smaller streams our byways which we would skillfully navigate in our search to find food such as fish, crocodiles and luscious crabs in the mud of the rivers, and wild boars and cassowary birds in the jungle along those rivers and streams. Once discovering and killing our prey, we would bring home the kill where it would be cooked with other food either from our gardens or with *pepeda* from the sago tree.

Once a month the elders would sacrifice a wild boar or cassowary bird to the spirits of the jungle to guarantee our hunting success and the health of the village. This animal sacrifice was given to the spirits accompanied by the blowing of a special bamboo instrument along with other loud noises and chants in praise of them.

There were special places in the forest where this sacrifice was offered. Such sacrifices to the spirits could be made only by the men who had been initiated into and participated in the spirit worship which took place in the *karwari,* the spirit house, where the proper ritual was learned and the spirit power was given to these men.

In respect for the spirits who had initiated the taboo, it was forbidden for those in attendance to sit with their legs crossed. One had to sit with his legs straight out in front of him for fear his legs would become paralyzed and perhaps even severed by the activity of the spirits during this ceremony.

If women or uninitiated men were in attendance, angered, the spirit could take the life of someone in the village. This was a very special occasion which provided health and security to the village.

During these hunts walking through the jungle, I was able to quietly observe the beauty of nature around me and the many different kinds of birds which flew about accompanying me on my path. Leaving our village, we normally had to walk through the jungle a pace before coming to the river where we had tied our dug-out canoes. These we would load up with our hunting gear, then strike off down the river in search of food. Our daily routine was to gather and hunt. When the jungle would no longer produce animals for our hunting needs or the sago tree for our main diet we would move on, searching for a new site.

Hunting, fishing, and working about the village were our daily routines. But I especially enjoyed going along with my elders on their hunting trips. When the hunting dog would yap and bay we knew it had tracked down some sort of animal such as a wild boar or a cassowary bird and was yelping to call us to come in for the kill.

If it was a wild boar, as a young lad I would run, climbing up the nearest tree for protection while waiting for my elders to come and kill it with their bows and arrows. Then, we would load it into the *perahu* to take it home. Hunted wild boars could be very vicious when cornered.

Other times I would join my elders in the dug-out, drifting downriver toward the ocean to look for crabs tunneled into the muddy banks of the rivers. Sitting silently in that dug-out watching the splendor of the jungle and floating by those trees with roots 3- to 4- feet high standing out of the water to accommodate the rise and fall of the tide, would often put me in a pensive mood. "How is it possible that the ocean water could rise, pushing salt water for miles up into the rivers, then fall again in the afternoon?" I mused. Within my heart, I would think, "This is impossible except that some Personality or Power directs its rise and fall."

As I grew, those thoughts also grew within me. "It doesn't make sense," I would think. "We are here, but how are we here? How did we get here?" I would ask my parents, "Are there other people living among us whom I have not seen?" And my parents would always answer, "No. We don't know if there are other people here in our world. The history of our past is not pleasant. We have heard there have been other people and other tribes, but intertribal wars and killings have decimated us. That is why we have wandered to this place. It is our feeling that we are now the only ones here."

After a time, I would ask again, "My father, my mother. I feel something strange is going on. How is it possible there is this beauty of nature around us with its many rivers, and beautiful birds? What is our origin? From where did we come? From year to year we follow, enjoy, and experience its beauty. The rivers bring us fish; the floods bring us crabs to eat; the forests produce fruit and nuts from which we survive. Who is preparing these things for us? Who has made them?"

My parents would answer, "Yes, there is Someone who made the world around us, but we know very little about Him, and we cannot go to His place." I would continue, "Why?" And the answer would always be, "Because we are defiled and impure; that place is clean—very clean—so clean it is not possible for us to venture there because we are also sinful.

"Because of our defilement, there is no possibility of us going there. For long years we have lived in this condition of defilement and it is too late for us to even think of getting to that place. Only those with clean hearts can go there."

Those words touched my heart deeply and produced a great sense of sadness and hopelessness within me—that there was no way I could even think of going there... or of knowing that Someone.

Some time afterward I again mused, "Is the sun that Creator who has brought this about?" Day or night if I would ask, the elders would caution, "Quiet. There is Someone listening. It is dangerous to speak like that." Meaning, the One who made the heavens and the earth should not be mentioned so casually.

Some days later, I heard the sound of an airplane passing overhead and I ran to my elders asking, "What is that plane?" They immediately replied, "There is an ocean in the sky with motor dug-outs originating there." I asked, "Those motor dug-out canoes...do they stop and tie up at places like this?" And my parents answered,

"There is a place beneath the branches of a large *beringin* tree where they stop to rest." "But who steers that motor *perahu*?" I asked, and my elders answered, "The angels."

I became afraid because I did not want the Creator to see me in my defiled sinful condition; my fathers had told me that those whose hearts were not clean and pure would be judged and punished. Hearing that, I ran and hid beneath the floor of our house among the posts on which it sat.

But I persisted. One day I asked my brother, "My brother, what took place in our past to make our situation like this?" He answered, "Quiet. Little boys should not be asking such questions." For a time I remained silent, but year after year I quietly pondered them until I was in my early teens.

Certainly we had our connections with our past through the spirits of our ancestors. These were called *"arwah,"* "the spirits of the dead." Only certain men— the shaman among our elders—were the mediators between the living and the dead. They alone were able to call on the spirits of the dead to come and make contact with those who were still alive. What these men uttered was, because of their intimate relationship with the ancestors, fearfully and unquestionably accepted by the people.

These men taught me that there had been a very special man who had visited them. His skin was like that of the Dutch, they said. He was a very special person, an "*anak dara*"—a man who had never had a sexual relationship with a woman.. Upon leaving, he promised he would return at the time designated. But no one knew when that would be.

We were told, "If we live right, he will return the sooner and bring change and prosperity to our village." This expectancy lay latent in the hearts of my people so that when they heard the Gospel and the story of Jesus their comment was, "Oh, so he was not from the Dutch; he was from the people of Judah!" He was often spoken of as the King of Peace because it was He who would bring peace and prosperity to my people. Interesting!

Hearing that, I immediately asked, "Where did that man go?" And I was told, "Probably to the land of the Dutch, but one day he will return." Hearing that, I asked, "What will he return in?" And my fathers answered, "He will return in a vehicle which he himself will create. We must wait his coming with patience and fortitude."

At that time, I had not heard a word about the Gospel, or heard the name Jesus. This story was passed down generation after generation by the elders of my people at Barapasi.

Chapter 6

Nature, My Teacher, Points Me to the Creator

At the age of 5 or 6, I was taken to Barapasi, the government center of the area, for the specific purpose of enrolling in the local Primary School. Even while going to school, I enjoyed going out to the river to fish. Every afternoon after school, if it had not flooded, I would sit on the sandy bank of the river with my fishing line, watching the tide water come in and go out. As my friends came by, I would ask them questions about how this all came about, why the tide rose and fell, and about this person who was to return.

Men from the local Dutch Reformed Church would mention the name "Jesus," but could not instruct me any further. So I would listen and ask myself, "Where does this Jesus live?" And I would ask my village fathers about the story which had been passed down generation after generation. Their answer was, "That Yesus about whom you ask is in the Netherlands. He will someday return."

Every time I would walk the paths back to my village of Marikai, I would observe the current of the river as it slowly made its way to the ocean. Because I was walking, I had time to think. "If the river floods and I am caught in that flood, I will certainly drown in its turbulent waters. And if I drown, what then happens to me?"

The trees along the banks of the river were full of beautiful birds chirping and singing; they seemed to delight in accompanying me as I walked along. This was nature—beautiful nature around me which could not have just happened. When I would return in the afternoon and evening to my village of Marikai during school breaks, the jungle would break out in a deafening array of sounds made by the various crickets and small animals.

All of this raised questions within me. "Is there a Personality who controls these creatures of the jungle as my elders mentioned? Who is He and has He compassion on me like it appears He has on these creatures of the jungle around me?" Since I was told it was impossible to be accepted by Him, I would wander on to my village deep in thought, but disappointed because there was no longer any hope for me.

Even before going to school at Barapasi questions about life perplexed me. I would reason, "There has to be Someone out there who made all of this and who is actively involved in sustaining it. If there is, He is probably watching every move I make. I seriously hope it is not the One who created it." These were my thoughts even as a young lad and often, when they surfaced, frightened I would run and hide in the bushes behind our house or among the posts on which our house sat. I did not want that One living up there in the sky to see me in my defiled sinful condition.

In addition to those fears and the questions arising in my mind as to who I was, and about who that Someone was who created me and the jungle around me, I had another fear about going to school. I did not want to go to school. I knew the teacher taught us in the Indonesian language, and I was not able to speak Indonesian. My language was the language of my village. "If I were to go to school," I reasoned, "anything the teacher said, I would not be able to understand and he would think me ignorant and probably get angry with me."

Furthermore, the relationship between the people of the village of Barapasi and my village, the village of Marikai, was not cordial. The Barapasi people were fearful of the magic of the people of Marikai and visa versa. When the people of my village of Marikai went downriver to Barapasi, before leaving the river to walk into the village of Barapasi they would beat their drums—the root of a certain tree—dong, dong, dong.

That sound would terrify the people of Barapasi who would fearfully welcome them into their village, making sure the children were safely out of the way so they would not say the wrong thing. If the people of Barapasi would offend the group from Marikai, the people of Marikai could place a curse on them using the power of their magic. We lived in fear of one another.

Another fear I carried into those early days in Primary School was my fear and embarrassment of being asked to pray in the Indonesian language. I could not speak Indonesian and I was afraid the teacher would ask me to go to the front of the class to open the class in prayer as was usually done. So, often under the excuse of needing to use the bathroom, I would run outside until I knew the class had started.

As I began my second year of Primary School, I became very sick. For several months my body, from the tip of my toes right on up to the top of my head, was covered with sores. We Papuans call this the "*kudis*" sickness—in which the skin of the entire body is covered with sores which become infected, probably from the intolerable itching, and exude a blood mixed with pus excretion with a sickening smell. This skin disease is highly contagious and anyone having any contact with such a person is fearful of being infected.

I went to the shaman over and over but received no help. I tried the local government health worker who repeatedly gave me shots; these also did not help. The more injections I got and the more pills I was given, the more the skin infection ravaged my entire body and I was miserable.

I had only one pair of school clothes—a pair of shorts and a shirt. When I went to school I would wear them; immediately upon arriving home, I would wash and dry them, and when dried would wear them again the next day. As I did not have any other clothes, I would shut myself into my small room waiting for my shorts to dry so I could wear them again. People distanced themselves from me because of the horrible smell from my body sores and because they were afraid my skin disease would infect them also. I was miserable in myself and contemptible to others.

Chapter 7

A Visit from One in a White Robe

My mother passed away while I was still very young and my father died when I was in second grade in Primary School. With both parents gone I began to feel as if I were being pushed aside with no one to care for me. I stayed with my older brother, Bastian. My body stank and my sores itched intolerably. I felt unloved, uncared for, and shunned by my people including my elder brothers. "Where could I run? What should I do? Was suicide in the river an option?" These were my thoughts.

One night, with these thoughts running through my mind, I fell asleep. Suddenly, I was awakened by a voice, "Karlos." I opened my eyes and screamed, for there standing before me was a man clothed in a white robe. I screamed again as he said my name a second time. "Karlos," he said tenderly. "I have a message for you. Within a short time a man will come with some good news for all of you." Though speechless I was totally conscious now, and with my eyes wide open I saw his hands and his feet as he turned and left me. Within a couple weeks, the open, draining, smelly sores over my body began to dry up and heal.

Several weeks later, I was bathing with some of my friends in the river when suddenly we heard the sound of what I now know is a helicopter. I shouted to my friends, "Listen! What is that sound?

Looking up in the direction of the sound, we watched as this large noisy bird flew over us, and I remembered the stories that my elders had told us. "In the days of long ago," they said, "stories were told of a large bird which would come flying over the villages looking for small children. When these were spotted, this large birdlike thing would swoop down and carry them away to kill and eat them."

"This is it," we said to one another. "It is looking for small children. Quick! Out of sight; let's hide in the forest." Then we ran and hid in the protective foliage of the jungle so as not to be seen.

From our safe hide-out among the leaves of the jungle, we watched as the helicopter landed in the village square (the ball field) at Barapasi. We waited for our clothes to dry, then dressed and headed in the direction of where we had seen that large bird descend. We dared not get too close for fear it would harm us, so we hid a short distance away beneath some banana trees to observe what might be taking place.

While we were all wondering and talking excitedly as to what probably was happening, suddenly my friend,

Othniel, shouted, "Shhhh. Don't move," he said. "A strange man just exited the door of that big bird. His skin is very different from ours. How is it that such a craft can arrive here without any paths and be guided by a man with strangely-colored skin?"

We edged closer, as it seemed the man with the strange skin was friendly to our elders who were gathering about the craft. As we moved in closer we could see the eyes of the man who had stepped out of the craft, and Othniel exclaimed, "His eyes are indeed like the snake's eyes." He said this because in the mythology of our people there is a story about a snake which could incarnate itself into a real person and we wondered, "Is this what we are seeing? Is this the one from The Netherlands for whom we are waiting?"

Shortly, we watched as the helicopter took off. Those around the craft said that it was going to my village of Marikai and we thought, "Why? Are there children up there for whom it is looking? Or, perhaps there are plans to develop the area to become a town?" After school that afternoon, we hurried up to our village of Marikai to see what might have happened there.

Conversation did not lag along the path. "Who was it who came in that large bird?" "Why did they come?" "Would they develop our village to become a small prosperous town?"

I was not the only one who was thinking and talking thus. All the people of Marikai were hoping that the visit of the helicopter would be the initial step in the development necessary to transform our jungle village into a small town with schools, stores, and government personnel—people with money. Such a transformation would ensure the resurrection and the return of our ancestors who had died. The story was that we would all be united again in this great, grand city. These were our thoughts and this our excited chatter as we made our way to our village that afternoon.

Upon arriving, we found the people gathered in small groups in front of their houses trying to synchronize their myths and the magic of a giant bird descending into their village with strange people having those "snake eyes." The word spread: This could be the coming of that Promised One who would bring the dead back to life and transform our village to sort of a kingdom where we would all live happily ever after.

"This was a certain fact," our elders said, "because when the helicopter landed, there was heard great rejoicing in and about the graves and places of burial throughout our area." Some of the men who heard this are still living and can verify this report.

The helicopter had returned to Barapasi and had taken aboard Mr. Imbiri as the guide to the village of Kerema, deep in the jungle along another large river further north and west of Barapasi. The plan was to locate both Kerema and Aumanefa, for these were the desperate areas needing assistance, both physical and spiritual.

This plan had to be temporarily aborted however, because Mr. Imbiri became disoriented in flight. He was used to seeing the villages from the dug-out canoe; not from an airplane or helicopter. With Missionary Scovill, then director of the UFM International in Papua, Mr. Imbiri guided us back to Marikai and gave the UFM International mission the freedom to use Marikai as its base of operation to move out to other villages throughout our area.

In a subsequent helicopter flight, Missionary Scovill came again, bringing with him the Yulius Hikinda family, recent graduates from the Sentani Bible and Vocational School of Irian Jaya, to open an evangelistic center in that area. Missionary Scovill relates the story.

> "With the Hikinda family on board, we frantically searched for a small somewhat open area where we could land the helicopter. After circling the area several times, we noticed an old discarded garden spot with a very run-down shelter in the middle. These shelters were very temporary and built to protect the workers from the sun and the rain during the day, and at times were their overnight sleeping shelters when they worked their gardens. From the air, we noted this garden was already taken over by tall grass and short bushes, but though risky, could serve our purpose.

The pilot looked at me with eyes which asked, 'Should we?" and I answered with a nod of my head as the pilot slowly and carefully set his big bird down in that old garden spot several hundred feet from that rotting garden shelter. We breathed a sigh of relief that we had not hit any trees, brush or stumps, and, with Yulius, walked through the long grass to have a look at the shelter.

I was disappointed. The sago leaf roof had rotted, allowing in both the sunshine and the rain; the small round poles which made up the floor about three feet off the ground, were broken, rotting, many were missing; the frame was leaning in such a way as to topple over with minimum movement inside.

I looked questioningly at Yulius. His eyes were bright with anticipation; his hands were already at work tucking in some of the missing poles that had fallen to the ground. I was disappointed and began to slowly shake my head thinking, "This can't work. I can't put a young bride in a place like this."

So I turned to him saying, "Yulius. This is the best the area has. Why don't you stay in the Marikai village with some of the villagers while working to provide a decent place for your lovely wife and she return to Sentani with us? When you have a place ready, we will fly her back here."

There was a long pause and finally it was Yohanna, his wife, who spoke. "Mr. Scovill," she said. "We have not come here to find a nice home complete with the conveniences of our culture. I cook over an open fire; I bathe and wash my clothes in the streams; we can live off the food we can find or that which is given to us. We have come here to serve together. Yulius is my husband; I will stay with him and we will build our home together." And Yulius' countenance reflected the joy and love for her as his new bride.

We left the garden, flew the short distance down river to Barapasi, and after saying "Goodbye, and God bless you," to Yulius and Yohanna, we left them to find temporary accommodations with the families at Barapasi and to pioneer the work in Marikai...which they amazingly did for the glory of God. And now Karlos can continue his story."

It did not take Yulius long to construct a very simple though temporary home for his family at Marikai. It seemed only a few days that it was ready, and the Hikinda family located there among the village people.

The welcome was warm; the soil loamy and rich for their gardening purposes and the location of their home next to several clean cool springs bursting out of the side of the little ravine—all a perfect setting and situation for this family. They were almost giddy with excitement at the potential of ministry and joy experienced living among my people.

All this was happening amidst the attempts of the members of the Dutch Reformed Church at Barapasi to hinder the opening of the evangelistic center in my village area. They failed largely because of the efforts of Mr. Imbiri who had welcomed UFM into the area. Though a heavy drinker and often drunk on the local liquor made from the sago tree, and though he was still a practicing shaman in the area and frequently involved in the worship of the spirits in the special spirit house of the village, Mr. Imbiri was also adamant in protecting the right of the mission and our church, the Evangelical Church of Indonesia, to be there.

When hostility would surface in the traditional Dutch Reformed Church regarding the presence of this new church and mission in the area, Mr. Imbiri would remind them that the Dutch Reformed Church had been in the Barapasi village for decades without any evidence of change in the lives of their members and without any attempt on their part to reach the Marikai village or any of the other villages in the area of his responsibility.

Though forbidden to do so by the leadership of the Dutch Reformed Church at Barapasi, after school on Friday we would walk up to Marikai to attend the Sunday worship service held in the Hikinda's home.

After Missionary Scovill came in the helicopter, we waited for evidence that this was the time when the promise of the resurrection of our ancestors would take place. We waited, and waited and waited, but no people came forth out of their graves in our simple cemetery. Gradually we realized this was a myth kept alive by our elders with no possibility of it happening. But there was an "eternal life" promised to us through the message of God's Word which we were beginning to hear.

When Missionary Scovill came with the Hikinda family, I was not present. After school with my friends, I had walked up to Marikai. I listened intently when Yulius would speak with his wife, but I could not understand his language. When my friend Othniel heard him speak, he said, "Hey! Incredible! This man is speaking English," though he was really speaking his own Sentani language with his wife.

During those first services, Yulius discussed with us the story of how God created the earth and sky from, what we now know, is the story of those early chapters in Genesis. He would speak in Indonesian, and since there was a man called Simson in league with the corrupt government personnel who knew some Indonesian, Simson would translate Yulius' lessons into my language of Marikai. When Yulius finished, Missionary Scovill would also speak and Simson would translate.

While this was happening, I would often drift off in deep thought, comparing and seeking answers to some of my questions about the earth and sky and who formed them. "Why had my parents wandered about this vast jungle to finally locate at Marikai? Were they being providentially led to this place so that I could understand this message?"

I remembered again the stories I had been told about a person who made the heavens and the earth, and I thought, "Yes, this is the same story; and it is true." As I began to tie together the fragments of these stories I became more convinced than ever that there was a Personality who made the heavens and the earth and that there was a Divine Hand guiding me in the direction which would lead me to that Person.

In search of that One, I worked up my courage to approach Pak Yulius to tell me more. "Pak Yulius," I said. "I was extremely happy to hear your story about the One who created the earth and the heavens. I would like to share that story with others. Please repeat it for me."

"Why do you want to do that?" Yulius asked me, and I replied, "I want to know more about the words which you are giving to us, and if later Mr. Simson does not come to translate for you, I'd like the chance to try. I would use our own tribal language so the people could understand."

Yulius' answer was very positive. "My little brother!" he said to me. "You make me very happy to hear you say that." After that, I was the one who would translate for him as he taught us the Words of Scripture. Because my people were hearing those words in their own mother tongue, a wave of genuine excitement and sincere interest swept through the village.

Chapter 8

Opposition Began: "Worms Will Feed on Your Dead Body!"

I was eager to learn from Yulius. I would take the lessons he taught and, following the foottrails of the jungle, I would head in the direction of the houses of my people, located deep in the jungle around us. As I walked, I pondered the question, "How is it possible that my people could truly know and love Jesus?" And tears would flow down my cheeks.

Yes, I knew the jungle well and those jungle trails over which I would walk oft-times in the darkness late at night. Even at that age, my heart was burdened because my people were caught in the net of spiritism—that power of darkness which closed their minds to the truth; they had not yet accepted Jesus as their personal Savior to enjoy the peace of divine forgiveness such as I had experienced.

After Yulius introduced me to Christ and I understood and received Him as my personal Savior, a great transformation took place in my own life and, with that transformation, an increasing burden to share that truth with friends. There was a distinct and inner force driving me. There was an extraordinary love and compassion birthed in my heart for my people which drove me to want to share the truth of the Gospel with them so they would not spend their eternity in hell.

I was not ignorant of the obvious: my people were not living as they should. My heart was deeply touched to the point where, when each time I would seek to share the truth of the Gospel with them, and even with my brother Bastian I would break into tears.

In an effort to make him understand, I gave him this illustration: "There was a man who built a house. That house was big and beautiful and built high up on posts to protect the family from snakes and other wild beasts. It was filled with the happy sounds of many children.

"But alas, those happy sounds ceased and turned to weeping because those children were tossed out of that house to the ground below. Every day they lived in fear of wild beasts. Every day the rays of the sun beat down upon them and the cold and rain of the night chilled them. My brother," I said to him, "those children are my people, and one of them is you, my dear brother Bastian."

In tears, I would press him to invite Jesus into his heart but he would always say, "Hey, little child. Don't cry. Don't weep for me. I'm okay. It seems you, little one, want to become like one of the elders in the church." And I would weep the harder for him because it seemed nothing would penetrate his heart and reveal to him his need for a Savior.

When Missionary Scovill came and explained God's Word to us, I would listen carefully. When he returned to his home at Sentani, I would hunt out those who had not been able, or had not come to the service, to share those truths with them. Each evening several of us young people—Hendrix, Gustaf, Othniel and I—would meet with Yulius for more teaching. Then the following day I would circulate within the village, sharing those truths with those of my people who would listen. Normally I would go by myself, because of this inner drive pushing me out to share with others the lessons I learned from Yulius.

I would go from house to house, often in tears, telling the story of God's love to us in the person of His Son, Jesus Christ. Though young, I was like a father who, seeing his children suffering out in the cold and rain with bodies now emaciated for lack of food and no longer able to help themselves, would plead with his children to come into the house where there was warmth and food, but they would not. As I pondered why, the tears would again flow. Often my older brother, tired of my pleas, and tired of my tears, would become angry with me. He did not want to hear any more of the Gospel.

Another of my older brothers, Permanes by name, would intimidate me saying, "Kairo, (he would use my village name), you are following a religious cult which is wrong. From this time forth, unless you change your mind and quit pestering us with this nonsense, we will no longer consider you our brother."

Because of this situation Simson, who was adamantly against this teaching and deeply involved in the spirit worship of the area, began discussing with the elders of my people how they might kill me. This was before I went to the Sentani Bible and Vocational School.

I was in fourth grade when I said to Missionary Scovill, "I want to go to Bible School." Missionary Scovill answered, "Karlos, that is a great desire, but you are yet a child in grade school. Finish your Primary and Junior High School first, then we will definitely consider it." Though I answered, "I'll do that," I was terribly disappointed that I could not attend right then to learn more of the Scriptures to be able to better explain the Gospel to my people.

When in fifth grade, I requested again to get into Bible School, but because of my age and level of education, I was again refused. In sixth grade, however, that desire grew within me to the point where I felt that if I could not go to Bible School, I did not want to continue my education. I had to study the Word of God.

I had seen some of Yulius' other classmates like Peterus Sokoi and Martinus Pulanda—all graduates of the Bible and Vocational School at Sentani founded by three missions: the UFM International, the RBMU International, and the Asia Pacific Christian Mission—and that is where I wanted to go. This desire was rooted deeply in my heart.

Opposition Began: "Worms Will Feed on Your Dead Body!"

After graduating from Primary School, and since the Junior High School had moved from Barapasi to another point down the coast to a larger village called Poiwai, I left for Poiwai in a *perahu* to attend Junior High there.

During those years in Junior High, my efforts at sharing the Gospel with my friends and classmates continued. When school vacations were given, I would make my way back to Marikai to continue my effort at persuading my people to accept this Good News. If they would reject listening to it, I would break out in tears pleading with them. When my own family rejected it, I would wander along the small winding footpaths of the jungle to other isolated places, finding people who would listen.

Often in the pitch-black of night I would grope my way back to where I was staying in Yulius's house, weary but happy to have been able to find those who would give an ear to listen. At times those of my village would come to me asking for more truth; this gave me great joy. Other times they would reject it and I would weep for them. Though still young, I was driven with the burden to share the Gospel with anyone who would listen.

During these times Simson would make contact with the elders of my people from other villages to discuss with them how to get rid of me in the community. Their consensus was that if they tried to harm me physically, the police would get involved, and they dared not attempt that. "Therefore," they said. "the only possible way to get rid of this menace is through our black magic." So, the elders and shaman of the people of the villages around like Sipisi would come with their threats. "Karlos," they would say. "Beware! Within a very short time, worms will feed on your dead body."

My answer to them was, "The Creator God is the One whom I worship. If He gives permission for me to die, I will die. Without His permission, you cannot harm me with your magic." Then I would attempt to share with them the Good News of the Gospel in Jesus Christ.

Attacks like this only further fanned that flame within me to tell the Good News. My attempts at curbing this effort because of their intimidation and threats only deepened that desire. The more I tried to resist, the greater the desire, until it would break out like a flood that compelled me to share the Good News and bring people to Christ.

Chapter 9

Opposition Intensified: Another visit from the White-Robed One

Then the helicopter came to take the Hikinda family back to their home village in Sentani for a six-month break. I was alone and that night while sleeping, I had another dream. In my dream I was again approached by the Person in a white robe who said, "Karlos. This is your calling and this is the message you are to keep proclaiming:

> *"Repent for the kingdom of heaven is near.*
> *'Prepare the way for the Lord;*
> *Make straight paths for him.*
> *Every valley shall be filled in,*
> *Every mountain and hill made low.*
> *The crooked roads shall become straight,*
> *The rough ways smooth.*
> *And all mankind will see God's salvation,'"*
> *(Luke 3:4-6).*

Having reminded me of that, he turned and left. I had no further doubt as to my task.

The next day was Sunday. Hikinda was not among us to call us to worship. So I sent out word, "Come let's gather for worship," and I spoke from Matthew 3 verse 3:

"A voice of one calling...said, 'Repent, for the kingdom of heaven is near.'"

Following the reading of that verse, I preached as I was told by the One dressed in white. The weeks following I continued to preach but because I was still a short skinny teenager, I stood speaking from the front of the congregation not from behind the pulpit. And the opposition increased.

The hopes and efforts of the older people who possessed the power of magic intensified. Their consensus was that they wanted me dead.

Once when I visited the home of a man, I witnessed these, the elders of my people who professed power in their magic, move through their spirit ritual to bring healing to a child who was deathly sick. All efforts were made to heal this sick child, but the more they tried with their various magical spirit rituals and incantations, the sicker this child became.

Finally I could control myself no longer! I jumped to my feet and shouted in the language of my people, "Yes, Father God. You are the Creator of the heavens and the earth. You are the one calling these families of the jungle to know your Son Jesus. On the basis of your great glory and authority, look upon us here (I was using our own

Opposition Intensified: Another visit from the White-Robed One

tribal language). Come and touch this child who is sick so that those who are gathered here will believe that Jesus Christ Your Son has all power and that He alone is the only proper One to be worshipped."

As I said those words in prayer, they all screamed in unison, "HAAA! You impotent little newborn child! Sit down! Sit down and shut up immediately." Then, one by one they climbed down the ladder of the doorway, screaming as they went, "How ridiculous that you, a child born just yesterday, could be brave enough to speak like that. Where is your God? Ours is the power known to be superior to all other powers—far more sophisticated and thus more trustworthy than any other in this area. If our power is not enough to heal this child, there is no other with stronger power upon which we can call.

"And you, child—how ridiculously brave you are to call on this Jesus, Jesus, whose name we are just now hearing. That Jesus has no power to heal. Our knowledge and ritual power can. Ours is the power proven in every expression of our chants and rituals which have been passed down generation after generation; your Jesus is a newcomer whose power is untried."

But I continued to call out that name of Jesus to heal this young child. After saying, "Amen," I opened my eyes, surprised to see there was no one there. Not wanting to hear more of that Name, each one had picked up his bush knife and his bow and arrows and left. I was left alone…with the child.

I turned to the sick child. "What about you?" I asked. "Are you confident that this Jesus can bring you healing?" Without hesitation, he answered, "I believe this Jesus has the power to heal me; please pray for me." After explaining more fully his need of salvation, I prayed for him, and yes, God answered by bringing healing to his soul and to his body.

This created a new expectation throughout the community. The sick would come; those not able to be healed through the magical rites of the shaman came to me and were healed. And the anger of these men against me intensified because they realized that healing in the name of Jesus was destroying their power and credibility. Among themselves they spoke of their dislike for me and said, "If we had known from the first that this would happen, we would never have allowed Missionary Scovill to come with his friends. He is a fanatic."

Mr. Simson was reported to have commented, "We don't have to receive that teaching. We thought these men were coming to benefit us—that through them our ancestors would rise from the dead and join us in building a great prosperous city. But the opposite is happening. Their presence and the proclamation of the message of this Jesus is destroying us and negating the power of our magic," and they all voiced their assent to Simson's words.

Finally, several of my older brothers spoke, "Let us find a shaman who has the spirit ritual so strong he can curse a tree and the tree will die. If that shaman can do

Opposition Intensified: Another visit from the White-Robed One

that to a tree, chances are he can use that same power to curse a man and bring about his death. The knowledge of a ritual that can do that is very powerful. He will be able to call upon his spirit power to forbid Karlos to mention the name of Jesus and Karlos will be muted. Or if he says, 'Tomorrow at the commencement of their worship service, Karlos will die,' it is certain that Karlos will die. The power in the ritual of a shaman of that order is potent. It has already caused the death of many people."

Thus the call went out to search for such a shaman whose curse was so powerful that I would die in the ritual of eating a coal from the fire. By eating that black coal, the blood of the man cursed would turn dark like the coal and he would die.

Eventually, such a shaman was found and the curse placed on me. Though I felt a deathly sickness come over me—the result of their curse—God spared me. They were unsuccessful in terminating my life.

Chapter 10

More Doubts, Another Visit: Call Confirmed

After graduating from Junior High School, I began to feel that perhaps I did not want to go on to Bible School after all. The head of the government on the local district level, the *camat*, pressed me to go on to High School. He was willing to use part of his government salary to send me to the capital city of Jayapura where I would attend the High School level training academy to become a civil servant.

While considering that, my Junior High School teacher, a believer and member of the national church formed by the Christian and Missionary Alliance, along with his wife, urged me to accept their funding to go to a Teachers Training School in Serui, a small town on the island of Yapen. Thus, I began to have second thoughts about my future and about leaving the ministry which I had once been so confident of pursuing. The temptation to pursue one of these options was very inviting. Position, status, salary—what else was important in life?

More Doubts, Another Visit: Call Confirmed

But one evening while I was sleeping, my friend in the white robe came again, "Karlos," he said, "look about you. Your area is shrouded in a fog of deep spiritual darkness. This day I want you to preach from Isaiah chapter 6 verse 8." And he left.

Since the Hikinda family had returned, very early the next morning I ran to Yulius' house and asked, "Pak (term of respect) Yulius. Is Isaiah chapter 6 and verse 8 in the Old Testament or in the New Testament?" Yulius answered, "In the Old Testament. Why do you ask?" And he reached for his Bible and read those verses to me.

> "Then, I heard the voice of the Lord saying,
>   'Whom should I send?
>   And who will go for us?'
>   And I said, 'Here am I. Send me.'
>   He said, 'Go and tell this people.'"

As I listened to those words, I was profoundly rebuked and my heart deeply touched. Those words so pierced the deepest level of my soul that at that moment I made the decision not to proceed with any thoughts or plans about further training in a government school where I could graduate with a position and a promising, adequate salary.

Without telling either the government official, the *Camat*, or my teacher, both who had offered to pay my way through the High School of their choice, I boarded a boat for Serui then made my way on a ship bound for Jayapura and the Sentani Bible and Vocational School where I had long anticipated attending.

Though I nearly grew up in a dug-out canoe, I had never been on a ship, so my journey was a terrible experience. I was seasick and vomited all the way to Jayapura though I ate nothing enroute.

Upon arriving, I had no clue as to where to go or what to do. Fortunately, friends in Jayapura from the village of Barapasi and the neighboring village of Bensor had noticed a ship from Serui in the harbor and in passing had said to one another, "I wonder if there might be some of our people on that ship?" So they turned back, saying, "Let's go see."

Immediately on saying that, they spotted me getting off the ship carrying my wooden suitcase, and took me to Kota Raja to stay with them. Yulius had used the Single Side Band transceiver radio to inform his friend, Martinus Pulanda, in Jayapura that I was coming. Martinus had searched all over Jayapura for me without success. Thus I went with the Peterus Bubia family to Kota Raja.

Since I remembered the address of the Sentani Bible and Vocational School, early the next morning, this family took me to Sentani. On arriving, however, we found no one there, so we headed directly to the market where people normally gathered in the morning to buy and sell their produce. We went around the market place asking, "Do you know a man by the name of Martinus Pulanda?" But no one could help us.

Finally I asked, "What about a man by the name of Henky Felle? Does anyone here know him?" "Oh, Henky

Felle," was the immediate reply. "Henky Felle is the one managing the Christian bookstore right over there." We were directed to the bookstore where I met Henky and told him the story of my connection with Missionary Scovill, who was also Henky's spiritual mentor.

It was Henky who then took me to the Scovills' home where we connected with Martinus Pulanda. I stayed with Martinus for several weeks until the Sentani Bible School opened its doors for the registration of new students.

Part 3

Formal and Informal Preparation for Ministry

Chapter 11

Head and Heart Preparation Continues

I entered the Sentani Bible and Vocational School delighted and enthusiastic to have the opportunity to study the Scriptures, hoping to better understand them and to become a more mature servant of the Lord in my witness to others. Even there my passion was to be able to better share the Word of God; my focus was: Study for the ministry.

During my first year at Bible School, I faithfully followed my study program as well as the daily work required of each student. Truthfully, I disliked the stern disciplined schedule required of us by our teachers from the west and, within my heart I protested, thinking, "This is a Bible School. The Bible teaches us to show love and compassion to one another, but, hey, this is more like the Army than a Bible School!" Obviously I did not understand that such discipline was required of me because it was molding my character to be a better lifetime servant of God.

During those Bible School study years, the overpowering desire to share the Gospel with others never left me. The teaching seemed to fan the flames of my desire to witness, pushing me out to find those who would listen. But I would suppress it and keep studying. Ofttimes I would go with Henky Felle to visit families, and to be counseled by him. Other times I went with John Marwedi to minister to the people in the villages on Lake Sentani who needed his care.

It was also during this time that I seriously began to attend the worship services of the Evangelical Church of Indonesia which met in the UFM youth center. In addition to my studies at the Bible School, my attendance at these worship services where good teaching was given also contributed to my spiritual growth.

After understanding the meaning and importance of the assurance of our salvation, I asked to be baptized in Lake Sentani during one of the baptismal services held by our local church. Some of my people from the Upper Waropen regional area living in Jayapura were astonished when they heard that I had been baptized by immersion and came asking me to explain to them the real teaching from Scripture regarding baptism. At the same time, I explained to them the Scriptures regarding how we could know beyond the shadow of a doubt that we are saved and thus children of God.

This was new teaching for them. Many had been baptized as infants and felt that was all that was necessary for their salvation, but within their hearts had no assurance of it and no personal relationship with Jesus Christ. Upon hearing the truth from Scripture many responded, repenting of their sin and waywardness and receiving the assurance of salvation. Many young people given to drunkenness and promiscuity were saved and others came back to the Lord. This greatly encouraged me to see God work within the hearts of my own people.

Among those who heard these truths was a man from my area whose name was Dorinus Dasinapa. He very much opposed this teaching because it so differed from what the traditional Dutch Reformed Church had seeded in his heart. And he made plans to catch and flog me, saying, "That Karlos! He is nothing but a young idiot! How is it possible for him to have anything beneficial to teach me who is much older than he? It is not proper that a small child should teach his elder!" And he waited for the chance to catch, confront and beat me, but that time never came. Eventually he, too, repented of his wayward lifestyle and was gloriously saved.

During those years at Bible School, after finishing our required work quota for the day we would have some free time when most of the students would race to the ball field. Playing soccer during my free time was okay, but I was moved to find a quiet place in the chocolate grove near the school to meditate and pray. When dinner time came, I would quickly shower and head for the dining room to eat with the rest of my classmates.

Often I was asked, "Where have you been?" And my answer was, "Oh, I've just been walking around in the garden." I did not tell them that I had sought out a place where I could get alone with God to pray. My heart continued to be deeply burdened for my people living in the bondage of spiritual darkness. I would pray, "Dear God, during this upcoming school vacation, please make a way for me to return to my home to minister again to my people there." During those times of prayer, I began to think of sharing this desire with Missionary Scovill, but I was too embarrassed to do so.

Then one day word came through Martinus Pulanda, who came to the dormitory to find me. "Do you want to return to your home this school vacation or not? Missionary Scovill has sent me to ask you." And I knew in my heart that this was the answer to my prayer. Without hesitation I said, "Yes, I do." "If that is your desire," he said, "be ready on such and such a day to return to Marikai in the airplane."

Thus, after finishing the end-of-the-semester tests, I boarded the small mission airplane and flew ninety minutes to Marikai, my home, to rest and to share the Good News with my people. Little did I know at that time of the confusion and consternation my arrival created among the elders of my people.

The common knowledge among the elders of the people in the area was that I was dead and no longer a threat to them. Therefore, when I stepped off the airplane, they were astonished that I had not died under the curse they had placed upon me—that I was very much alive.

Head and Heart Preparation Continues

I immediately began visiting from house to house both day and night, sharing the Good News with my people who were living in drunkenness and debauchery, ancestor and idol worship and making incantations to the spirits in the spirit house in the forest as they invoked the evil spirits' power to produce their magic .

It was forbidden for any woman or uninitiated to go into that house. It was called, "*Garinuma*" meaning "The Hot House," or "House of the spirits," where the youth were initiated and taught the chants and rituals to make contact with the world of evil spirits. These special initiation ceremonies were held two or three times a year for the youth to learn the rites and incantations passed down from generation to generation.

Not all the lessons were evil. There were some lessons and rituals used to catch fish in the streams and rivers as well as incantations which would bring animals of the jungle to the hunter for him to kill. But they also were taught the rituals and magic useful in putting a curse upon someone to cause his or her death. My heart was crushed to note that many of the youth of my age—many of them my friends and fishing buddies—had already participated in these ceremonies, initiating them into the world of spirits that had power and authority over them in their daily lives.

My visits to the houses and villages continued for over a month and a half. Each evening, people would row their dug-out canoes from the distant villages of Barapasi, Sipisi, Bariwaro, as well as the occasional group from the Lower Waropen regional area, quite a distance from the Upper Waropen regional area where I was located at Marikai.

They would tie their dug-out canoes to the reeds and bushes down at the river, then in excited festive groups, walk up to where I would be waiting for them. There was an obvious hunger to hear these truths from the Scriptures given in our own mother tongue.

So encouraged and excited was I to be able to speak to them about these eternal things that taking time to find something to eat was furthest from my mind. I felt it more important to give priority to the need of the soul rather than to the need of the stomach! They had poled their dug-out canoes for hours because they wanted to hear words which they had never heard before and I did not want to disappoint them.

But the time for me to return to school at Sentani too soon arrived and I knew I must find my way back by small ship. I knew too well that the months of June and July were the months of rough seas with huge waves making it nearly impossible to get out to Serui where those larger ships dropped anchor.

One day while struggling in prayer to know what to do, Yulius received a call on the Single Side Band transceiver radio. "Tell Karlos to be ready on such and such a date; an airplane will be there to pick him up."

"Incredible," I thought. "Here I am a simple little

penniless jungle lad but my Heavenly Father has noticed my need and sent the airplane." To me this was indeed a miracle. As scheduled, I left on the airplane for Sentani to return to Bible School.

Chapter 12

Relief from Those Hunting Dogs!

After leaving on the mission airplane, I was told that the elders of my people slipped into the "Gari" house, the spirit house, to discuss a strategy for killing me by using their magic. Men from Bariwaro, Sipisi, Marikai and even some from the Baudi tribe who lived further in the jungle came to agree on the plan.

They took charcoal from the fireplace and while munching those coals in unison pronounced a curse on me. They then spit into the fire and shouted, "Just as this wood has become charcoal, so may Karlos become like this—a burned out piece of wood. May he die in Sentani and not return again to his place here in Marikai." They then repeated their ancient incantations.

In the airplane flying to Sentani, I felt my body become very weak and limp with both my hands and feet beginning to cramp. When this condition did not change upon my arrival at Sentani, I went to the doctor for medical help; this too did not produce any relief. The

Bible School teachers also gathered with Missionary Scovill and Henky Felle and it was Henky who prayed the prayer of Romans chapter 16 verse 20:

> *"The God of peace*
> *Will soon crush Satan under your feet.*
> *The grace of our Lord Jesus be with you."*

He strongly felt that I had indeed been placed under an evil curse by the elders of my people at Marikai. Still each night I would dream of being surrounded and attacked by hoards of evil spirits. They would come at me from the land; they would descend upon me from the air; they would ascend from under the ground, like fluttering moths and bats, making every effort to strangle me. I would sit up in terror on my bed at night feeling my hands and feet in cramps and cold. I could get no relief.

One Sunday I shared a brief testimony of this with the congregation meeting in the Youth Center at Sentani. Missionary Scovill sensed what was happening. Immediately following the service, he called the leadership of the church together to pray for me.

Their prayers were passionate. Again Henky Felle counseled me, "Strengthen your faith; God wants to deliver you of this enemy." It was true, though I reacted negatively because I was very depressed at my situation. In my heart I said, "Strengthen my faith; how does one do that? You, Henky Felle, are not feeling what I am feeling. It is I who am feeling this terrible sickness!"

Out Of The Dark Triangle

Yes, I was in a depressed state of mind and in the midst of that depression I wondered if I should yield to their pressure and cease to speak any longer of that Good News; however, the opposite occurred within me; the motivation to do so increased. The greater the temptation to cease speaking of Jesus, the greater was the tug of that Divine Hand directing me out to tell the Good News.

In my heart I said, "This is like a man hunting a wild boar. When the wild boar hears the hunting dogs behind him, he runs with all haste to get away from them. Dear Father, release me from these dogs—this tyranny of spiritual darkness and fear. I choose to follow the calling you have placed on me, to live or to die sharing the truth of your Word."

And I was released. The Holy Spirit moved in to heal, to encourage and to strengthen me. I was delivered. My skies turned blue again. My heart felt again the peace and joy of ministry.

Six months later I was on my way flying back to my village of Marikai. Stepping out of the plane, the elders of my people who had placed the curse on me were again astonished and muttered among themselves, "What is the source of Karlos' power that our rituals and incantations are not able to destroy him?"

When I made my way through the village, these men stood in the doorways of their houses shaking their heads, muttering in my language, "He's back alive. Our incantations had no effect on him. What is that power? Seriously, from where comes the power that he uses?"

I heard later that after I had made my way through the village, the elders met again to discuss my case. "This is too important a situation for us in which to fail," they said. "If the first level of our effort fails, we must move to a higher level of ritual. We must destroy this young man. It is very dangerous for our area if we allow his teaching to go on." They began to carry their bows and arrows and their bush knives to take my life. But amazing! Whenever I would meet them on the path, or in the ordinary routines of life, they had no power to do any harm to me.

During my school break, their rituals moved to a higher level of power and passion. Through their incantations, they attempted to send poisonous snakes, the cobra snake, into Yulius' house where I was staying. One snake tried to climb the steep steps of Yulius' house but Yulius saw it, and killed it with a club.

After I returned to Sentani to complete my Bible training program, for two straight months every day when I went to the garden to do my required work I was confronted by these aggressive snakes which tried to frighten me. Though I would kill them, the next day there would be others that had come in to harass and frighten me. We were convinced these were snakes sent by the elders of my people—a part of the curse placed on me—to poison me and take my life.

Finally I called my classmates to come pray with me. We asked the Lord to shatter the power of the evil one sending those snakes to harass us and He did. After we deliberately placed that garden area under the authority of the Lord, the snakes did not return.

Chapter 13

Death Keeps StalkingMe

Six months later, I was back at Marikai during another school break. Word of the curse placed on me had become known throughout the area. Thus when I stepped off the airplane, astonishment and confusion reigned. It was obvious that the second effort of the elders of my village to destroy me through poisonous snakes was unsuccessful. So these men met again to rise to a new level of power and ritual which hopefully they thought would accomplish their evil desire to rid the community of me and the power in the name of this Jesus.

Secretly they brought their fetishes and buried them in the yard around Yulius' house where I was staying. Each night when I would lie down on my bed to try to sleep, I would hear footsteps walking around the house, the clear sounds of deep breathing, and someone pushing at the door of the house. Several times I grabbed my flashlight, raced to the door and shined the light in the direction of those noises. But the noises stopped; there was no one there.

Three months later two coconut trees and three fruit trees in the yard, for no obvious reason, began to wilt and die. The door and the walls of the house were attacked by hordes of ants and termites. It seemed that though their power could not touch the man they wanted, it mobilized the insect world to reap havoc on our house and yard. Their efforts were totally powerless to touch me.

Following that episode and because of it, three of the men prominent in the spirit world came asking, "Child, in truth we have failed. But we want to ask you again, from whence comes the power that you, Yulius Hikinda, Peterus Sokoi and Missionary Scovill use? It is far more effective then ours." I answered quoting Mark chapter 16 verses 15-18.

> *"He [Jesus] said unto them, 'Go into all the world and preach the good news to all creation. Whoever believes and is baptized will be saved, but whoever does not believe will be condemned. And these signs will accompany those who believe: In my name they will drive out demons; they will speak in new tongues; they will pick up snakes with their hands, and when they drink deadly poison, it will not hurt them. They will place their hands on sick people and they will get well.'"*

Then I explained the meaning of the verses to these men in our own language. They listened respectfully, pondered them with heads nodding, and fell silent. Then, without further comment, they stood and one by one made their way down that pole ladder into the inky blackness of that jungle night, but also down into that dark fog of spiritual darkness in which our area was shrouded.

I continued to be harassed and intimidated in my dreams by the more subtle evil spirits impersonating insects and fluttering about me like moths and bats. At other times, I would see in my dreams men approaching me with arrows which they shot at me, but I was never hit. Their arrows fell short of their target.

One day while I was preaching, an older man approached me in the church with an arrow in his bow aimed at me. For some strange reason, another Power seized him when he tried to release it and the arrow fell from his hand as he fainted.

In another dream, someone grabbed me by the throat and threatened me with the sharp weapon we make from the bamboo. I cried out in my dream, "My God lives; He will save me from your attempt to kill me." In my dream, I forced myself loose from the hand of this one with the weapon, leapt to safety, and woke up. When I woke up both my hands and my feet had gone numb and void of any strength. Yulius' wife witnessed my condition and cried with me.

A month later, I was with a group of young men overnighting in the home of the Dani school teacher, Stephen Wonda from Mulia. In the middle of the night, these youth saw my entire body glow like red hot coals.

The people of my culture at Marikai believe that such a glow is a sure sign of the person's imminent death. It did not happen!

Threats of this kind would be accompanied by a shaman in our native dress having his headpiece decorated with crocodile teeth or the feathers of the cassowary and bird of paradise. In his hand he would carry his bow with a bundle of arrows, sending the news to all villages in the area that a young man by the name of Karlos would soon leave this earth. This is what was done to me.

When I was told that I was to die in keeping with the ritual of this curse placed upon me by the local shaman, I said to the church, "If I die, don't weep for me. Accompany my body to the grave site with spiritual songs of praise because I have gone to be with my Heavenly Father."

Several days later I left again to return to Bible School, still bothered by the contact of the curse, with my hands and feet limp and often cramping. Since this increased in flight, I was taken to the Immanuel Hospital at Mulia to be checked out by Dr. Jerry Powell, the UFM doctor there.

After a thorough physical, Dr. Powell said, "Karlos, don't give way to the thought that you are sick. I don't believe that you are. There is nothing wrong with you that I can discern. I can find no symptoms which convince me otherwise. I have never examined anyone with a sickness such as you say is bothering you." He said that after thoroughly checking me with all the latest technical equipment of his skills.

Though my hands and feet were still numb and cold and I was feeling sick, since the doctor said he could find nothing wrong with me, I climbed back on the airplane and went on to Sentani. I still felt sick but since the doctor had said I was all right, I set my heart to believe him and continued my studies. I did not want to surrender to whatever it was making me sick. I was very much strengthened by the verses found in 2 Corinthians chapter 12 verses 7-10:

> "...there was given to me a thorn in my flesh, a messenger of Satan, to torment me. Three times I pleaded with the Lord to take it away from me. But he said to me, 'My grace is sufficient for you, for my power is made perfect in weakness.' Therefore I will boast all the more gladly about my weaknesses so that Christ's power may rest on me. That is why, for Christ's sake, I delight in weaknesses, in insults, in hardships, in persecutions, in difficulties. For when I am weak, then am I strong."

Chapter 14

A Power Encounter at Sea

Following our third year of Bible School, all the students were sent out to practice in the field what they had learned in the classroom. I made my way back to Marikai to continue my ministry there. Again they came from the surrounding villages of Barapasi, Sipisi, Bariwaro and other villages in the Waropen area to hear the words of Truth from Scripture. My heart was encouraged to see the desire of my people to hear the Word of God, and for their sick to be healed through our prayers for them.

A year later I returned to SAKIJ to finish that training and in the afternoon enrolled in the Teachers Training School which would enable me to teach the Scriptures in the local public schools. After graduation I had to get back to Marikai, and since the airplane could no longer land at the Marikai airstrip because of lack of maintenance, I looked to take a ship—but I had no money!

In a prayer group that evening, I mentioned this as a prayer request and Pastor Koirewoa prayed, asking the Lord to give me a ticket to return home. Within that group was a man who heard that prayer and after the service came asking, "Who is this Karlos who needs a ticket to return to his home in the Waropen area?"

"It is I," I replied. And he said, "Fine. I will be responsible for that ticket." He took me to the ship, purchased my ticket and sent me on my way. And I had marvelous opportunities to share the Gospel with many on that ship.

Arriving in Serui where the ship docked, I was faced with another problem. I had no money to pay the small fare to take a dug-out from Serui to Barapasi, about six hours across the ocean. So I prayed again. And God sent another man from the Baptist Church to urge me to go to see the *Bupati*, the leading government official for the area who was also a believer, and it was said, "He wanted to meet me."

So screwing up my courage, I went to his office. He gave me a very warm welcome and asked, "How are you? I am very happy to meet you. I have heard of your burden for ministry among your people at Marikai." To which I replied, "Thank you, Sir. I am fine, Sir."

"And how is Mr. Scovill?" he asked. I answered, "Missionary Scovill is now located at Sentani and news of him is also good." Missionary Scovill was a personal friend whom he greatly appreciated.

Then he asked, "When are you going to your village?" A bit embarrassed I had to reply, "I'm ready to go now, but must make contact with a boat going across." He immediately understood what I was saying, reached down, pulled out a drawer of his desk and said, "I am not able to share the Gospel like you, but I can and will help you with your fare to return to your village." And he gave me far more than enough funds for that trip across the ocean. That very same afternoon I boarded a small motor *perahu* going to Marikai.

In the middle of our journey across the ocean the sea turned sullen and rough with waves so huge that we could not continue our journey. So we docked on the beach of a small island to wait out the storm. In the boat with us were several passengers of the Muslim faith. Having beached our boat to wait out the storm, all the passengers began to work the power of their magic to quiet the waves. There was one passenger who held a chunk of wood with some leaves on it with which he struck the water while muttering his incantations. But the waves only increased and put us all in very much danger.

Watching this, I felt the strong urge to pray. So I stood to my feet, raised my hands toward heaven and prayed, "Praise your name, O LORD God, because you are the Creator of this universe. It is You who has made the heavens and the earth and everything in it. This sea is under your authority and control. I pray that you, my Father God, will calm this sea so that those who have just tried to use the power of their magic will witness that you, Jesus, are Almighty God, the only One worthy of our worship." And I sat down.

A Power Encounter at Sea

To the astonishment of all, the sea immediately was calmed and though dusk had fallen, we crossed safely into the mouth of the river which would take us to Marikai. As we motored into the mouth of that river, the wind picked up again bringing with it ocean waves higher than before, but we were safe having reached the calm of the river.

Seeing this, the passengers of the Muslim faith along with the police who were also Muslims, asked, "Who is this young man who prayed?" My brother who was steering the boat, said, "He's my younger brother."

Because darkness had fallen, we overnighted on the beach with several families who were fishing along the coast. This was my opportunity to share the Gospel with both the passengers and the village men who were there on a fishing expedition. I smiled, because some of these were from my village and always ducked away when I wanted to share the Good News with them. Here they were—my captive audience.

Chapter 15

Worshipping in Our Own Mother Tongue

Having graduated from both Bible School as well as from the Teachers Training School, I arrived back in my village and culture. With all my heart I wanted my ministry to reach out to my people in a way which they could understand and appreciate. I felt there was no better way than to conduct our worship services in our own vernacular language. In this way the worship could truly touch their hearts and could be felt in the very soul of the worshipper. I was not wrong.

We began singing our hymns in our own language, accompanied by homemade musical instruments—guitars which we made ourselves out of logs, the big one-stringed bass cello using nylon fishing line for its one or two strings. This was very attractive to the people and drew them into the services with an air of excitement, heretofore not experienced in the worship of our Lord.

It was a new experience for them to understand the Scriptures and to feel the presence and joy of the Lord in their midst. Too, this manner of worship powerfully influenced other church services in our area. Church was not a dead, dry, negative experience; it was a happy, joyful experience with even the women and children singing at the top of their lungs. I was thrilled!

Unfortunately a letter went out to the leadership of our church, the Evangelical Church of Indonesia, with copies to the UFM mission headquarters at Sentani, that I was introducing a new kind of wild worship into the services. A copy of this letter went to Missionary Scovill to warn him that it would be inappropriate that I attend seminary training as UFM was planning.

After getting the letter, both the church and mission leadership flew into Marikai to see the situation and to make their own evaluation. They quietly observed our worship style and they watched the enthusiasm of the youth and the women heartily and joyfully singing. The next day they called a meeting to discuss the matter. It was Jim Larkin, head of the UFM mission at that time and one of the teachers in the Bible School at Sentani, who spoke first.

"Beloved friends in Christ," he began. "If, in fact, Karlos is teaching a style of worship which is inappropriate, I, his teacher, am at fault. But from what I am observing, my teaching has not been inappropriate. This visit is far different than our first visit some months ago and I am astonished.

"During our first visit, there were relatively few

who attended, and fewer who joined in the singing. This time I have noted that young and old and both men and women are enthusiastically joining in the singing of the hymns in their own language. I am greatly encouraged."

Then, the head of the church walked to the front of the congregation and said, "Whatever style of singing during worship is appropriate in this area and within your culture, enjoy it as long as it is not contrary to the Word of God and our church constitution. Due to the number of different tribes and cultures represented within our church, we must be flexible in allowing the worship liturgy which best expresses the soul of that culture." The congregation clapped their approval and appreciation and that was the end of the problem;

Chapter 16

Challenges to Become Self-Sufficient

I needed money for soap and I needed funds for clothes and transportation. The apostle Paul supported himself through his tentmaking efforts. I would do the same, so I tried various means to support myself in ministry.

The Agricultural Department of the government was distributing chocolate trees to the people of Marikai to plant, then to market the large chocolate seeds to increase their income. It seemed a good investment so I obtained some of those trees, made a small garden and planted them. The chocolate gardens of the members of our congregation thrived in the rich soil at Marikai and produced abundant fruit and income. Alas, mine died—all of them!

I tried to catch fish and sell salted fish. This seemed a very profitable and marketable effort in our culture. With the income from this I could support my ministry. That effort also failed.

Then, UFM gave me two drums (400 liters) of kerosene to sell for a profit which I could use in supplying my personal needs. That also failed because I sold on credit which I was powerless to collect!

Then, I thought I would try to raise chickens to sell both the eggs and the meat. Yulius and I made a big chicken pen and stocked it with two roosters and about ten hens with the rationale that when reproduction reached a hundred chickens, we would begin marketing them to obtain some ministry support. Though the chickens of the members of the congregation produced well and increased their income, mine caught a disease and within a short time all died.

Finally, since the government was giving out fishlings, I dug a reasonably large pond near Yulius' source of drinking water and put my fishlings there, determined this income-generating project was going to produce for me. Several days later a huge rain created a flood which came rushing down through that tiny gully and wiped out my fish pond with all the fishlings. Not one fishling was left in that pond.

I was devastated—until I realized this was God's way of reminding me that I was not born to be a business man. I was born for a different purpose, the glorious purpose of serving Him and being totally dependent on Him for my daily needs. And that is the way I have tried to live during these years of ministry.

Part 4

Seminary and Commencement of Ministry

Chapter 17

The Whisper Was Clear: Lampung, Lampung

Several months later I received a letter from Missionary Scovill, who at that time was in Jakarta, inviting me to pursue further Bible Studies in a seminary outside of Papua. This would indeed add to my theological training but would, as well, enlarge my experience of living and serving the Lord outside my relatively comfortable village life in Papua.

After weighing the matter and seeking the mind of the Lord in prayer, I felt this invitation was confirmation that His will for me was to proceed; I made this known to the congregation and to my family.

Hearing this news, the congregation as well as my family forbade me to go. Some cried; some were confused. My uncle asked, "Why do you have to go there? Today, I am in good health but tomorrow, who knows? If I get sick and die, I will not see you again."

These words pierced my heart and I joined others of

my family who were weeping. That night I again struggled in prayer to know God's will for me. Again, I felt the quiet whisper of the Holy Spirit urging me to go. So, on January 2, 1992, I left Serui on a ship bound for Jakarta. Even on the ship I had many opportunities to witness, as well as the joy of praying with some of the passengers.

Arriving in Surabaya, I was met by some of my Papuan friends. Together we boarded a bus and left for Jogjakarta known as the University City on the island of Java, and the location of the seminary I anticipated attending.

However, during the two weeks I stayed with my friends there, the feeling within me that this was not the school I was to attend increased. So I was taken to Jakarta where I stayed with the pastor of the local Ebenhaezer church of The Evangelical Church of Indonesia, our own denomination in Jakarta. He was also a professor in the branch seminary located in West Jakarta.

I diligently made an effort to make the necessary adaptation to a city situation like Jakarta—a city so full of every kind of pollution with a very depressing hot, humid climate that I felt it nearly impossible to stay. I was not used to living in a cement jungle, nor hearing the continuous roar of vehicles, nor breathing the exhaust fumes of cars and buses on the streets.

The singing of the birds, the sound of the rivers and streams, the chirping of the crickets and other insects at night, the smell of the fire and the freshness of clean air—all were a part of my life in Papua.

Because of the change in climate and the pollution, I took sick with a high fever and chills, a very bad cough, and nausea of the worst kind. Thankfully because of the blessing of the Lord, I was able to get over it.

I began to participate in the visitation program of the congregation, praying with and sharing the Word from family to family. I was also active in a ministry with the youth and involved myself in the Sunday School program teaching the children. However, the biggest hindrance to my ministry was my market-place level of Indonesian which the people could not understand. This, plus my black skin and kinky Papuan hair, made it difficult for them to accept me. Often they would sneak outside to play with their friends during Sunday School.

However, I felt the strong hand of God with me. I would eat my meals in the small eating stalls along the road. When paying for my food, often someone would slip up to me and say, "My younger brother. You don't need to pay; allow me to take care of it."

I would make a telephone call and when I went to pay, the manager of the telephone stall would say, "There is no charge; someone has already paid for it."

When riding on one of the local buses, often I did not pay. As I went to pay the fare, someone behind me would say. "Don't. Your fare has been cared for." There were those who said, "Sir, you don't need to pay. You are from that distant Papua. Allow us to assist you by paying."

If these were acquaintances, I could understand, but these were people I had never met who were coming to help me in my need. I knew beyond the shadow of a doubt that my Heavenly Father was with me and His hand was pressing these men and women whom I had never met to be His instruments in my life. I was truly humbled by their kindnesses, and by His grace.

Through all of this, I began to feel that Jakarta, too, was not the place for me. The climate was inhospitable; I had no money with which to exist in a big city; my Papuan friends were far, far away; my black skin, kinky hair, and marketplace language made me feel out of place. And above all, the main food of my village diet—the sago soup mixed with our delicious swamp greens and crab meat—was unavailable. Mine was the village life; my self-image was deteriorating. I made the decision to return to my village in Papua. But I had a problem: I had no money for the ship's fare to return!

So I phoned the UFM office in Sentani. Their answer distressed me further. "Oh," they asked. "Who is paying for your ticket?" And I had no answer because I was too embarrassed to ask UFM to pay.

Aware of my situation, Pastor Bambang called me and said, "Karlos, you came here to Java for further schooling, did you not?" "Yes, Sir," I replied, "but I cannot hold on any longer here in Jakarta. I must return to my village."

The Whisper Was Clear: Lampung, Lampung

To this, Pastor Bambang said, "Karlos. Think first! If you have come here to learn, don't think of returning to your home. Missionary Scovill will soon return from his furlough; wait and talk this through with him." And I waited.

While waiting, I filled out entrance forms to three different seminaries. All of them accepted me, but I had no peace of heart about going to any of these well-known and well-staffed evangelical theological schools in Java. Then, my friend Helman called me to his home to discuss the matter.

"Karlos," he said, "Why don't you consider going to the satellite branch of the Evangelical Theological Institute of Indonesia in Lampung, Sumatera. (The mother school was in Jogjakarta where, at first, I had intended to go). "Maybe the Lord could use you in a church-planting ministry in that area."

Immediately I felt that this was in keeping with my thinking. While studying the Word there, I could be used of the Lord to pioneer a church-planting effort for my church, the Evangelical Church of Indonesia. I went and talked through the matter with Pastor Bambang.

He was not convinced; in fact, he was disappointed that my thinking was moving in that direction. "Did you not come to Java to attend the mother seminary in Jogjakarta?" he asked. "Why do you now want to go to its satellite school, still under development? Was your direction to the satellite school in Lampung, Sumatera, or to the mother school in Jogjakarta? Why are you wavering in your thinking?" he asked. I responded by saying, "I have a strong urge in my heart to go and visit this satellite seminary in Lampung first."

I began to pray, "Heavenly Father, if it is your will for me to go to seminary in Lampung, please confirm this in my heart." And the whisper, "Lampung, Lampung, Lampung," was His answer. So I made plans to go to Lampung in South Sumatera to see the school for myself, but I had no money.

So I prayed, "Lord, I have only 20,000 rupiah (US$2). If this is your will, give me the sign of someone who is willing to assist me with expenses along the way. I have no money for fare and no money for food." Though penniless, following that quiet whisper within me, I made my way to the terminal of the bus which would take me to Lampung.

Chapter 18

To Lampung and Return with My Rp. 20,000 Intact

Once in the terminal, a man whom I did not know came up to me, inviting me to eat with him. "Thank you, Sir," I said, refusing his invitation. But he insisted, "Come. Take a plate and dish out some food for yourself." Again, I refused, but thanked him kindly.

He continued to press me to eat. "Come," he said. "There is no problem. I'll pay for it." Because he seemed to be sincere in his insistence, I finally took some food. When I sat down beside him, I noticed that he had prayed, asking God's blessing on his food before eating.

After praying myself, I opened up our conversation by asking, "What is your particular work or profession?" "Oh, me," he said. "I'm a pastor with the Bethel Pentecostal Church here in Indonesia."

"Praise the Lord," I said, "We are brothers in Christ," and we chatted together about ministry while enjoying our food. From that encounter I knew that a Higher

Hand had prepared food for me through this servant of His, and my spirits lifted. Maybe God was truly in this adventure I had begun. My 20,000 rupiahs (US$2) was still intact!

I climbed on a bus headed for Merak, the ferry dock at the western end of the Java island, with intent to board the ferry to take me the two-hour ride across the strait to the Sumatera island. I sat next to the driver, who was from Makasar in Ujung Padang. We chatted amicably as he wildly wheeled that rusty old bus along the congested highway. When I went to pay my fare, "Don't," he said. "You don't need to pay. We are Indonesian brothers, are we not?" My 20,000 rupiahs was still intact!

I crossed the strait on the ferry, and boarded a bus for the two-hour ride to the city of Bandar Lampung. Arriving there I was totally confused. I had never been in this city before. "Where do I need to go and how am I to get there?" were my inner questions. So I found a policeman and asked him, "Sir, this is the first time I've been in this city. Where do I find the Gedung Air?"—the address I had been given.

"Oh," he said, and pointed me to a small bus, "If you want the Gedung Air address, you must get on that bus and go in that direction." Providentially, on that bus was another evangelist from Papua who took me to the address. It was the address of my friend, Helman, who had pressed me to visit the Seminary there in Bandar Lampung.

I went to the house and greeted the maid who came out and opened the gate to let me in. "Who would you like to see?" she asked. "I have come to speak with the parents of my friend, Helman," I replied.

Confused, she answered, "There is no one by that name who lives here." So I said, "His sister's name is Sumfa." "There is no one here by that name, either," she answered. "But Helman gave me this address and told me that his sister's name was Sumfa," I stammered. "Sorry," she said. "No one by those names lives here."

Confused and somewhat annoyed, I didn't know what else to say, so I stumbled to the gate, then returned. "Mr. Helman's wife is from the Batak tribe and his father-in-law's family name is Sitompul." I said.

"Oh," the lady of the house, who had joined the maid, responded. "My son's name is 'Amen,' not 'Helman.' He indeed does live in Jakarta and is married to the daughter of Mr. Sitompul." It was then I learned that my friend Helman was called "Amen" there in the home, and his sister, Sumfa, was called "Soneta." Those formalities over, I was invited to stay overnight with them and the next day I was taken to the home of Mr. Sitompul, Helman's father-in-law.

Speaking with Mr. Sitompul—a dear man of God, walking the streets of Bandar Lampung, and pondering my future, I sensed that whisper growing stronger in my heart to pioneer a church-planting ministry in Lampung and the surrounding villages. Though I was not aware of it at the time, this burden was to grow. God was placing the entire island of Sumatera upon my heart.

I returned to Jakarta convinced that I was to prepare myself to enter into my college-level Bible training program there in the city of Bandar Lampung while taking the Gospel to some of those distant isolated villages where the Word had never entered.

And the 20,000 rupiahs (US$2) I took with me to Bandar Lampung, I brought back intact—unused—to Jakarta when I returned.

Chapter 19

Ministry: Kedondong

In August of 1992 I returned to Lampung with my friend, Anton Gultom, who also wanted to attend the satellite seminary of the Evangelical Theological Institute of Indonesia in Lampung. After settling into the dormitory, each Friday and Saturday we would move out into the community looking for strategic places to open a base for our evangelism efforts. This was normally preceded by a time of fasting and prayer, seeking the direction of the Lord for our evangelistic and church-planting ventures.

Oft-times, when the rest of the students would return to their various activities, I would hide away in a classroom to pray for the Lord's specific direction as to where and how to begin a ministry of reaching souls in areas known to be fanatic and violently opposed to our message.

After one such time of prayer and fasting, we decided to visit an area called Kedondong and climbed on a village bus heading in the direction of the marketplace. Once there, since Anton was a Batak with the family name of Gultom, we asked if there were any Gultoms in the area. To our delight there were, and we jumped on a motorbike taxi and made our way to his home several kilometers up along the mountainside. Upon arriving, we learned that he was not there and, according to his family, would not return for several months.

When we knocked on the door of his home, two lovely young girls opened the door. Seeing this black man from Papua, they ran outside to fetch their mother, who was working some distance away in the garden. Incredibly, while we waited outside, their father, who was not to return for several months, returned. We were warmly welcomed—Anton because he was a part of the Gultom extended family, and I, because I was a messenger of the Gospel, and this family was a Christian family.

They were adamant that we immediately begin a weekly Bible Study in their home. So as inconspicuously as possible, since this was a highly intolerant Muslim populace, each Sunday evening we met for fellowship and study of the Word. Each week the group grew with others who, professing faith in Christ, joined with us. The people of the Muslim faith did not yet know that I was an evangelist.

One such weekend after our Bible Study and time of worship, suddenly I felt very weak and broke out in a cold sweat. So I slipped into the room where Anton and I were staying to pray. Seeing my situation, Anton said, "Friend. You look sick. What is the matter?" And I answered, "I feel a sense of impending danger. I do

Ministry: Kedondong

not know what is going to happen to me!" "If that is the case," Anton responded, "it is better that we not use the same path on our way out of the village. We will find another."

We found a small footpath through a coconut plantation and made our way to the main road where we got on a small bus taxi to return to our dormitory at the school. That next week, we learned from one of those who attended our fellowship, on the evening we had left, a small group of Muslim fanatics had waited with their sharpened bush knives to secretly dispose of us. Our God had protected us.

Another time we went to Kedondong to minister. As usual, I went to the river to bathe, and as I was bathing I noticed another man approach the river to bathe. When he saw me, he quickly grabbed his towel and ran. It seems that he had not yet bathed, but when he saw me he ran and reported to the police that there was a black man in the area.

The following week, Anton and I were called in to be questioned by the local police as well as by the military police in the area. "What is your business that you come weekly to Kedondong?" they asked.

Both of us were stressed-out having to explain our frequent visits to the area, but the Lord enabled us to do so and our ministry and the group, mostly from the once-Christian Batak tribe, continued to grow. God has his own delightful ways of working and ours was the joy of seeing our numbers increase as well as seeing the spiritual growth in the lives of those men and women of our fellowship.

We also began reaching out to the Chinese businessmen in the small town of Kedondong. Intentionally, I would often drift into their stores looking for a chance to share Christ with these families.

After friendship was established, I would begin by discussing the price of merchandise in their store. "My friends," I would say. "Your efforts have produced a very fine store to meet the needs of the community here. But I note that there is one piece of merchandise which is missing which is far more valuable than all the other items. And perhaps we, from the furthest eastern province (I was black from Papua), have been sent here to share that news with you."

Astonished, they would ask, "Do you need something like transportation or something else from our store?" I would respectfully answer, "My father and my mother. Among all the various items sold in this store, you and your children are of immeasurable value in the eyes of a God who loves you—far more valuable than any of the riches in this world." Then they would ask, "Are you a Reverend?" And I would answer, "No," because I knew if I said, "Yes," my witness would be rejected.

Normally and cordially they would continue, "Come! Come! Let's shut the doors of the store for a few moments and discuss these things in our home behind this building." And we would retire to their home behind the store.

Once there I would read and explain the story of the treasure hidden in the ground as found in Matthew chapter 13 verses 44-45 and say, "My father, and my mother. Mining companies are spending trillions of rupiahs in their efforts to discover and to extract the gold and silver from the bowels of the earth in Papua, but God is seeking you, my father, and you, my mother. He offers you that eternal treasure of salvation and the joy of a personal relationship with Him." And many of those Chinese businessmen responded with joy, opening their hearts and receiving Jesus Christ as their Savior.

Chapter 20

Ministry: Karang Sari

With the Kedondong group now the responsibility of Anton, I visited other small towns and villages and befriended a young man on the outer fringe of a village who was raising chickens and fish. At one time, his wife had been a practicing Christian, and they were interested in studying the Scriptures. Being a bit isolated from the nearest village, I felt this would be a good place to open a Bible Study with them.

This man had built a small two-story house of local wood materials. The family slept upstairs, and I was given a spot on a bamboo bed next to the chicken pen on the ground floor. I helped him dig up their garden where he planted the *singkong* (tapioca) plant for their daily food. This was my attempt to adapt to the simple community way of life in hopes I would be accepted in the community. In the evening we would study the Scriptures and pray by the light of the kerosene lantern.

Several days later, I heard an announcement from the nearest mosque, "You men and women of the Muslim faith. Beware! Beware! There is a black man who has entered our community. This man is definitely on a mission to make us Christians. Words which will lead you astray have entered our area. Beware! Beware!" The next morning I returned to my dormitory.

The following week, I went back to our Bible Study with that family in their field. The nearby village was about half a mile from the larger village of Karang Sari from where children would come to see this strange and frightening black man. But I made friends with them and in time was able to have a small Sunday School with them.

At ten o'clock one night, in the light of their torches, a group of men approached the house of my friend there in the garden. "Where are you from? And what is your purpose in being here?" they asked me.

I answered, "I am from Papua. Jonathan is my friend, and I have come to help him." I didn't dare say I was a Christian or from the church for fear of being chased out of the area. Hearing this explanation, they seemed at least temporarily satisfied and left. We continued our times of Bible Study and prayer but a bit more secretly.

Two months later, a man came offering us a good price for a house on a piece of land which he wanted to sell for only 3,000,000 *rupiahs* ($300). This obviously was a good investment for the future, so I phoned the data to my missionary friend in Jakarta who sent us funds to purchase the property. This became my base of operations, the beginning of a second center for evangelism and eventually a church-plant in that area.

When I first came into the Karang Sari village, all the women ran into their bedrooms in fear, peeking out at me through their bedroom windows. Others would run and hide, waiting for me to pass their homes, then ask one another, "Why does that black man come to our village? Where is he from?"

But I stuck it out in my house in the village, trying to get close to the people through the village efforts of doing things together; eventually I was accepted as a bona fide member of the community. I also made every effort to become friends with the Muslim leaders of the village though they did not know I was a religious man of the Christian faith. I continued to have my Bible Study with the Jonathan family.

About six months later, there was a young child in the Islam school in the village who became deathly sick. Late one night his family came requesting me to help them. They knocked on my door, and when I opened it they asked, "Does *Om* (uncle—a term of respect) have any magic rituals from Papua?"

"Magic ritual concerning what?" I asked somewhat surprised. "Magic rituals which you could use to make our sick child well," they reluctantly responded. Then, the older brothers cut in, "Our younger brother is very sick. Please come and help us."

"Oh," I said, somewhat baffled as to what to do. "I'm neither a shaman of magic ritual nor a doctor with medical skills." But suddenly there was a strange movement within me and a whisper reminding me that this could be God's opportunity to share the Gospel with these people so I said, "You return to your home and gather your extended family. I will be coming shortly." They immediately left and called all their family together to wait for me.

Upon arriving, I saw the hopelessness of the situation. His breath was coming in short quick gasps as a gagging noise came through his voice box, "Aagh, aagh, aagh." There was no hope.

I stood up and said, "My friends of the Muslim faith. I cannot help this child," I said. "But there is one about whom your Muslim book, the *Al-Qur'an* speaks, who can," and I began to explain from their *Al-Qur'an* about this one called "*Isa Almasih,*" Jesus, the Anointed One.

"He is the one who made the lame to walk, the blind to see, the deaf to hear and the dead to be raised to life. His power has not changed even to this day. Come my friends. Let us pray to this One to heal your son. This *Isa* is the Word who lives. He became a man like us. He does not bring a religion; He brings salvation to those who trust in Him. Who is this *Isa*? It is Jesus Christ and we will now pray in the power of His name."

I lifted my hands, and in a clear voice prayed, "My Lord God, the Creator of heaven and earth. Come heal this child so that these people here will know that you, *Isa*, the Anointed One, are God and the only one worthy to be worshipped." While I prayed all the people who had gathered in that room quietly left. I was standing alone with the child's parents and his immediate siblings.

I turned to them and said, "Do you believe that this Jesus can heal your child?" Some answered, "We hope so." Others said, "It is the will of God!" I briefly explained again God's plan of salvation offered to them. Seeing that the breathing of the child had returned to normal, I, too, requested permission to leave, and returned to my house.

Once in my house, I took every precaution for my safety for I was worried that I may have offended my Muslim friends who would come threatening me.

Early the next morning the parents knocked on my door and said, "Last night about 10 o'clock, our child became completely well." "Thank the Lord," I said. "Our Lord Jesus heals!"

The news spread. Soon many were bringing their sick to my house asking me to pray for them and this became my opportunity to share the Gospel. If they could not come to my home, I went to theirs. During the day I visited those at a distance, riding the motorbike taxi; during the evening hours, I went from house to house in our own village, riding my bicycle, to explain the Gospel. Many declared their desire to believe in Jesus.

Ministry: Karang Sari

Sometime later I heard there was a Batak police officer at the local police station. Since I enjoy the Batak people (and I was learning their Batak language), I went and introduced myself. I knew there was a good chance that he, being of the Batak tribe, was probably at least a nominal Christian.

After we met and became close friends, he opened his heart, confiding to me the need for help in his troubled marriage. During this time our friendship grew and I spent time counseling and praying with them. But he still felt he had to have some sign, some evidence that I was really a genuine servant of the Lord.

The first sign given to him was when an unknown person delivered a sack of rice to him. He was totally astonished. The second was the invitation to him and his mother who was sick to come visit me in Karang Sari to be prayed for. We prayed together and discussed the Scriptures.

As they prepared to leave, I noticed it was clouding up to rain so I said to them, "Better wait a while because it is going to rain." But he replied, "No, I've got work at the office waiting for me; I must go." So I prayed again and they left. But strangely, as they went, it rained heavily in front and behind them, but they were not rained on in their journey home and they were amazed.

The third sign was the total transformation experienced in their marriage. Convinced at last, they accepted me as a servant of the Lord and came surrendering themselves totally to the Lord as a family.

He also introduced me to another Batak family, the Sidabalok family, whose husband lived far from the Lord. He was a brutal man—to family and to friends and known for such throughout the community.

At one time he had attacked a policeman with a club, knocking him out. My friend, the policeman, wanted to shoot him, but didn't because another policeman grabbed his pistol. Now my police friend wanted me to minister to the Sidabalok family, which I did, and he with his family were gloriously saved and transformed by the grace of God.

Because of this transformation, the Sidabalok family opened their home for worship services which eventually outgrew their home; we built a church behind their home to accommodate the numbers. Sadly, Mr. Sidabalok died several years later, but the church-plant at Sukoharjo remains and thrives to this day.

Another time, as I was pedaling my bicycle around looking for possible contacts with whom to witness, I pedaled past a woman who was returning home from her teaching routine. Feeling the whisper of the Holy Spirit to speak with her, I stopped and waited for her to catch up to me. When she did, I greeted her warmly, asking where she lived.

I could see she was astonished and a bit fearful as she pointed to her home a short distance away. "Don't be afraid, Ma'am," I said. "My skin is dark, but my heart is white. May I ask where your husband is? I'd like to speak with him."

"He normally comes home about 5 o'clock in the afternoon," she answered, to which I replied, "May I come by to visit him when he returns home at 5?" And she answered in the affirmative.

That encounter raised questions within her: "What is that black man doing here?" "Why did he stop to speak with me and why does he want to come to our home?" That afternoon at 5 o'clock I was there explaining to her husband the gift of salvation offered in Jesus.

His wife, who was listening to our conversation in an adjacent room, connected that conversation with a dream she had had several weeks before. In her dream she had seen her house and yard covered with snow. When asking herself what the meaning of that dream might be, a gentle voice from the midst of that snow had answered, "This beautiful white snow covering your home and yard comes from the mountains of Irian Jaya." (Irian Jaya is now called Papua.)

This dream prepared her for my strange visit (I was from Papua) and subsequent explanation of salvation when she with her husband received Christ as their Savior and became active members in the new congregation at Sukoharjo.

Part 5

Marriage
Mercy
And More Ministry

Chapter 21

A Broken Marriage and a Bankrupt Ministry...Almost!

I had a house and I was enjoying ministry, but I was alone! As the ministry unfolded, I was attracted to a young lady in my class. Though we had little contact and no relationship whatsoever, little by little I became aware that she was a young lady of Javanese parentage and that her village was just up the road a few kilometers from my home in Karang Sari.

I felt she was just a friend, but why was she so often in my thoughts? And why would she notice my times of prayer and fasting to prepare food for me afterward? From the stories I began hearing from her friends and her family it seemed that she was attracted to me as well. When asked about my relationship with her, I would always say, "She's just a friend. There is no special relationship between us."

But it was very strange; I had never experienced such a feeling before. She was different from all the other girls and from the comments I was hearing from others,

I felt she was experiencing the same feeling for me; I had heard that she had once said to her friends that she wanted to marry a man from Papua. Was she kidding, or was she serious? I was a Papuan, and from what I was feeling, she was sending signals of love to me! It was not long until we began to fall in love and began dating.

Not having had any experience in this area of life I felt it strange, even difficult, to express this love, so I did my best to put distance between us to the point where she wondered if I were a normal male. In the end we went to Jakarta for counseling with the Scovills at which time Suarti, for that was her name, shared with Mrs. Scovill that she questioned whether Karlos was normal. Certainly he was not responding to her overtures of love like other young men. It seemed he had no desire toward the opposite sex.

I laughed when I heard that for I had plenty of sexual attraction toward her, but I had put a fence around myself so as not to be driven to the physical. My principle was: no marriage; no touching. I wanted to protect her as well as myself since we were both in ministry.

One time, to test me, she had said, "If you are a brave young man, try kissing me and I will know that you love me." To which I replied, "If that is your thinking, then I think you better look for another boyfriend." And I was serious. I also realized we really did not know each other so took seriously the counsel of the Scovills, who sent us out with their funds to see the sights of Jakarta.

We went to Taman Mini; we went up to the very top of the national monument called Monas. It was there that I said to Suarti, "Look around you at the beauty of this city. The houses in my village in Papua are far different than the houses here in Jakarta. My house in my village is like a chicken house. The walls are made of the branches of the sago tree, with little privacy. The roof is made with leaves of the *rumbia* tree (type of palm tree). When it rains at night, we are wet until morning. Why would you ever want to marry and follow me to a place like that?" I was testing her because I knew our future would involve ministry in places like that.

Suarti paused a moment then said, "Jakarta is full of every kind of pollution; the air is so dirty I could never endure living here. Besides, I too, am a simple village woman."

I continued, "My house is in the middle of the dense jungle. The evening silence is filled with the sound of the crickets. The place is dark, without lights. There are hordes of mosquitoes. Why would you want to go there with me?"

She cried, then said, "Karlos. You are human; I, too, am human." Meaning, "I, too, am a simple village girl—born and raised to live in a village setting—and I have no desire for anything else."

I asked again, "Is there not someone better than I for you to marry?" Her answer was an emphatic, "No! I am in love with you and that makes all the difference!" We returned to Lampung but continued to put a reasonable distance between us in our relationship.

Sometime later I said to her, "If in fact we eventually want to marry, what is your response to the obvious that I am penniless?" Her response was immediate, "If our courtship is in the will of our Heavenly Father, He will open the way for us to marry by providing the means!" And she was right.

A short time later, through one of His servants, the Lord provided sufficient funds which allowed us to have a very simple but impressive wedding service followed by a festive marriage celebration. This event was a real testimony to our friends in the village and throughout the area.

As is normal in the Javanese culture, after marriage we stayed with her parents for two weeks, then moved to my home in Karang Sari to begin our ministry together. On one reed mat we slept, we ate our meals, and if we had guests we would sit on that one mat as well.

But alas, it was not long until our marriage relationship began to deteriorate, probably because of our very different dispositions and certainly because of our different cultures. I, as a Papuan, was very direct, aggressive, even abrasive; she, as a Javanese, was very kind, considerate and sensitive. I would say one thing, and she would understand something far differently than I intended. Predictably, the result was arguing which led to division and fighting between us.

I would come home late at night from a tiring day of ministry only to find the door of my house locked. Since she would not open the door for me, I would borrow my Muslim neighbor's crowbar, force open a window and enter through the window.

We fought over food. There were several kinds of Javanese food which she prepared which smelled terrible. I could not even stand the smell of it let alone eat it, so we fought about food.

Sadly, in the midst of this confusion and fighting, we no longer took time to pray together. Every day we quarreled. When I would come home late at night feeling weary and hungry, she would say, "Eat your Gospel message. See if that fills your stomach!" It was true; I was ministry-focused but my family was suffering. I was the man in the house, but not the husband aware of and meeting my wife's needs. She felt betrayed and lonely.

In addition, we were the gossip of our friends and the local community to the point where our ministry friends and church leadership felt we should leave the area because we were such a poor example to the other believers in our congregation.

Finally, because of our ruined testimony, we were asked to leave our home in Karang Sari and were placed on disciplinary probation for six months. We rented a house in Lampung and we were told to forego ministry to focus on the healing of our marriage relationship.

I tried to hold out—restraining my emotions, but they would erupt and I would lose it in a fit of anger. I would try again: same thing—anger and fighting between us until one day, in a fit of anger, I beat her. That was all she could take. She grabbed our child and without telling me, left for Jakarta, some seven hours travel time away via bus, ferry and taxi, to talk with the Scovills, our mentors.

She traveled all night, arriving early in the morning to knock on the door of the Scovill home in Jakarta. When they opened the door, they were shocked to see at their door my sobbing, bruised wife with a black and blue face where I had hit her.

Not long afterward, I telephoned the home of the Scovills in Jakarta. "Hello," came Missionary Scovill's voice on the phone. I answered by saying, "Hello. Good morning. How are you?" Mr. Scovill replied, "Fine. How are you and what's the news of your family?" Not knowing my wife was there with them, nor that they knew about our marriage situation, I answered, "I'm just fine."

Hearing that statement, Mr. Scovill turned his sights on me. "Don't lie to me, Karlos. You say everything is, 'Fine, fine with you and your family,' but your wife stands here in front of me, her face black and blue from the beating you gave her."

Shocked was I, and my heart shouted, "Oh, no! Let me die from embarrassment! My wife has told them all!"

A Broken Marriage and a Bankrupt Ministry...Almost!

Mr. Scovill continued, "Tomorrow I am bringing your wife back to you in Bandar Lampung. Give me the respect of waiting for us in your home!" The next day after a full day's drive Missionary Scovill, with my family, arrived at our rented house in Bandar Lampung. But my heart was still hard as nails, and my head as hard as stone.

I was thinking, "This is it for me; my ministry is finished. I'll never be able to return to our home in Karang Sari." And that only further ignited the anger in my heart toward my wife.

When she walked through the door, I shot out at her, "Why did you run? You are the one creating chaos in our family and destroying our ministry. Now you are brave enough to run to the Scovills with our problems. Shame on you!" I said this thinking that it was about time the Scovills realized that she was the one destroying our ministry and forcing us out of our home at Karang Sari.

Mr. Scovill just sat there listening. By the time I had finished venting my fury on my wife, she was crying. After a significant pause, Mr Scovill turned to speak... not to my wife, but to me. "Karlos," he said. "It is obvious that though a messenger of the Gospel, you are far from this God whom you introduce to others. You are rebelling; the one who rebels is called a rebel. And that rebel is you!

"I was under the impression that you as a servant of God, in genuine humility, was being used by Him to bring many people to the Lord. But it appears that while you bring others to the Lord, you yourself are far from Him. I am shocked to see and feel your attitude. Karlos, you are rebelling against God, and you need to repent." Mr. Scovill began to weep unable to continue his rebuke of me. All of us fell silent.

I looked around me. My wife was crying; Mr. Scovill was crying. It was then that I realized it was I alone who was not feeling any sense of remorse—that this was because of me—that this was my fault.

That truth slowly filtered through my head and reached down into my heart. Shocked at the rebellion I now saw within me, I hung my head in shame and I, too, began weeping.

"My spiritual father," I said to Missionary Scovill. "You are right. You are so right. Help me. Please help me. I need your help."

My pride broken, my heart freed of its anger and rebellion, in all sincerity I turned and asked the forgiveness of my wife and of the Scovills who had mentored my family and who for years had assisted us in ministry. Now, they struggled with us again—to re-build our marriage.

We almost separated; I almost ran back to my village in Papua. We almost sacrificed the Bible Studies and evangelistic opportunities God had opened up to us and went home rejecting God's call upon our lives. But praise God, I can testify that today our family is different from those early years. Our relationship both within the home and within our ministry is beautiful. God has indeed done a miracle in bringing precious harmony out of the tears and trauma of those early marriage years. We praise Him.

Yes, I must say that today I understand and must confess that the problem of those years was more mine than hers. The confusion and hurt in our home was caused by me. I had not accepted her as God's gift to me to complete not only my life but my ministry. I felt that I was the only one who could be right because I was serving God. I had forgotten that serving God also included serving my wife!

With the counsel of the Scovills, our family has been restored. Every morning with our two children we gather to have devotions and to pray together. I am beginning to understand the needs of my wife and she also is seeking to understand my disposition as well as my burden for ministry, and strongly supports me in her prayers.

For a time I felt God could not use us any longer as His sharp instruments. But in the midst of our storm, He has restored our family and continues to use us in sharing the Gospel with those who do not know Him and who come seeking our ministry. Many are repenting and accepting Christ as their personal Lord and Savior.

Though I am not worthy, God has not rejected me. We have experienced His tender mercies in the healing of our marriage. Though unworthy, He has reached out, raised us from those dark confusing days, and made us able to serve Him once more. I am conscious that God's call upon us is not dependent upon our abilities but upon His will, His call, and His daily grace given to us. There is nothing about which we can be proud!

Chapter 22

Our Ministry is Being Monitored

Our ministry continued in the field and it appeared that from the very first we stepped into the district of Kedondong, we were being followed. Even the small Bible Study groups we led were being monitored. Harassment and other efforts to make us stop were obvious.

One time when I went to Sukoharjo, suddenly three men appeared to observe the number of Christians meeting there. Their response? "Oh, this is the result of Karlos' ministry." When I went to Karang Sari, they would appear, observe and comment, "Oh, more of Karlos!" When we opened up a ministry post in Pagelarang, they also came. "Karlos is here also," they commented. The same thing happened when we began a Bible Study in the village of Padang Ratu. The believers in those places informed us that at the Muslim school my name, Karlos, was the first on the list for whom they were preparing to silence through death.

Several times they came with their rifles to gun me down but the Lord protected me; I had left before they arrived. At other times they would wait, but I would arrive late. Tired and bored in waiting they would leave and I would slip in after they had left. I knew they were seeking me. I also was aware that they came as spies telling the people of those villages not to mention their efforts at trying to destroy me. However, since I had good relationships with the villagers, they would quietly warn me that unknown men had come seeking me.

One afternoon they came and overnighted in the small mosque to await my coming or going. That afternoon after our Bible Study I had a strange feeling in my heart not to go home that night, so I slept in the home of my father-in-law. Early the next morning, a strange group of men was seen leaving the mosque and returning to their village.

Half an hour after they had left, I arrived at my home where the people of the village came and reported this to me, even though they were forbidden to do so. In the end, I went and reported the incident to the police who came soliciting information from the people to enable them to chase down the leader of this movement.

Three days later, a member of the Intelligence Department of the Police boarded a small village bus. He was dressed in plain clothes like the other passengers so no one knew he was a member of the Intelligence Department. During his journey another man, who happened to be one of the group seeking my life, was chatting with others in the small bus, boasting that he was a member of the military. Indirectly, he was threatening the driver with a gun in his hand, frightening the rest of the passengers. Our friend from the Intelligence Department began to suspect something was amiss. "If he is truly a member of the military, he certainly would not be acting in this way," he mused.

So, instead of exiting at his intended destination he went on with the bus, accompanying this one who was frightening the other passengers. When the bus arrived at the Police Department, our police friend from the Intelligence Department exited the car and ordered the driver of the bus to proceed with all the passengers into the Police Department complex. Once inside, he reported the incident to his supervisor who ordered his police staff to surround the bus, making sure no one escaped.

With the vehicle surrounded and the passengers still inside the bus, the head of the police questioned the man. "Are you indeed a member of the military?" he asked. The man replied, "Yes, I am." "Would you please show me your identification card?" he ordered. The man answered, "I have none!" "Then, what is your military identification number?" he was asked. That he could not answer either, and he knew he had been caught.

In the end, the police arrested him. When questioned, he admitted that he was out looking for a black man by the name of Karlos. He was beaten because of lying about his identity, and his case was transferred to the military to process. For several weeks after that, there was a member of the police sent to guard our house in case there were others who would come seeking me. But after that man was arrested, we were not disturbed again.

However, there were continued attempts to harass us in hopes this would silence me. One time they brought four lumps of dirt from the cemetery and placed them in front of our house, then returned to the Muslim school and fasted for three days. That night we saw the lumps of dirt glowing like red-hot live coals. Because I knew the origin of this was the power of darkness in the area, while praying God's protection on us I went out and scooped up the dirt in my hand.

When I picked up the dirt, I felt a strange numbness creep up that hand which, after we prayed, went away and my hand became normal again. The dirt we took and burned, calling on the name of the Lord to protect us from those attempts to harm us.

Several days after that, the man who came placing the dirt in our yard, with intent to put a curse on us, went insane and a week later he died in the Muslim school where he taught. It seems that the ritual used in placing a curse on us through that dirt returned to haunt him, and he passed away. This is in keeping with Mark 16 verses 17-18.

About a week later, three policemen went to that Muslim school in our village and, pretending they did not know, asked, "Why is that black man living in this village?" The staff at the Muslim school said, "He is dangerous! We have tried over and over to use our magic to silence him, but our magic is not working. It seems he has a magic far more powerful and sophisticated than ours. Our rituals and incantations are powerless against him."

One evening, several months later, I felt a strange feeling come over me so I slept outside our bedroom close to the door. About 2 o'clock in the morning, I heard a knock at our door: knock, knock, knock. I jumped up and looked out the window by the door to see who it might be but there was no one there. I lay down again and shortly heard the knocking again. Again, I jumped to my feet and looked outside, but there was no one.

When this occurred a third time, I opened my eyes and there beside me stood a man in a white robe. He stepped about three paces toward me then vanished. Because I was now wide awake I stood at the window wondering what was going on. It was then that I saw about five men run away from our house into a nearby rice paddy and vanish. I woke my wife and told her what I had just seen.

Several days later, some of the people from the village told our neighbors, good friends of ours, that a group of men had come with intent to kill us, but ran away when they saw several soldiers in white robes complete with their weaponry, standing protectively in front of our door. This is completely in keeping with Psalms 34 verse 7 which says:

"The angel of the Lord encamps around those who fear Him. And He delivers them."

There is no question in our minds that they were angels of God sent to protect us, and we bow in gratitude to Him.

Chapter 23

Burned Out!

About six years after locating in Karang Sari, I received an invitation to attend a meeting along with the other religious leaders of the government area we were in, the district of Waringin Sari Timur. During those years we were able to finish our house with permanent brick walls, a new roof and a cement floor to replace the dirt floor. Adjacent to our home, through the gifts of friends who supported our ministry there, we were also able to build a simple but nicely built small church where we were happily meeting.

Respecting the invitation from the government, I made my way to the office but, to my surprise, no one was there. So I waited in the large waiting room of the building until the head of the government in the area, the *Lurah*, arrived and called me into his office. Once in his office, he began a very emotional tirade prohibiting us from any longer worshipping together at Karang Sari.

When he finished, I said, "Thank you, sir. If that is the prohibition, I request you put in writing the following:

It is completely forbidden for the Christians at Karang Sari, to meet together for worship on Sunday." But he was not brave enough to do that. He knew the law was on our side.

While we were still in his office speaking about the issue, hundreds of people began to arrive. They came in trucks; they came in cars; they came with hundreds of motorcycles—all shouting, "That black man is evil; he's a monkey; he's an infidel. Come, let's kill him and celebrate together. Let's make meat balls out of him. Give him to us; we'll take care of him!" It was clear they wanted my blood and there was nothing I could do. I just quietly sat there smiling...and waiting.

As the noise of the thirsty crowd increased, two policemen came into the large room where I had been asked to wait. The one in civilian clothes drifted out to mingle with the masses while the one in police uniform came and stood beside me, presumably to give me some protection. At the same time three trucks loaded with angry people made ready to move in the direction of my house. My wife and child were in that house but I was helpless; there was no one I could send to tell them to move out and get into hiding.

Screaming their rage, the masses continued to pressure the police to release me to them. "This is the country of the *Panca Sila*," the police said. "You can't take the law into your own hands." But the crowd turned nasty and yelled back in unison, "Who are you to tell us what to do. You, too, take the law into your own hands; we have lots of proof!" and they picked up stones to throw at the police.

As the masses continued to gather, the tension sharpened, and here I was, separated from my wife and child, with death staring me in the face and the masses intent on moving in the direction of our home to kill them and to burn down our home.

It seemed the situation could not be altered. I looked around at the masses with eyes of compassion and tried to smile, but they scowled at me with anger written in their eyes and on their faces. They were out for the kill, and were increasing in numbers and threats. So I hung my head and prayed, "Lord, help me and my family still in the house. If this is your time for me to die, Thy will be done."

Shortly after praying, I was startled to feel a change come over the situation. The masses full of sadistic intent began to slip out of the office. The tension in the air diminished and though many were standing alongside the road, I stood and walked through them without incident. This had to be a God-thing.

Arriving home, I briefly told my family what had taken place and urged them to leave Karang Sari immediately to take refuge with her parents several kilometers away until this crisis was over. It was obvious the masses would be coming to burn down our home and church. Hopefully I could protect myself, but protecting my wife and child would not be as easy.

"Why are you saying that?" my wife persisted. "Because my heart is not at rest" I said. "There is danger out there for us. Tonight is the night we will probably experience what we have hoped would never happen. Come, please leave immediately. If you don't want to go to your parents, take refuge with my friend in the police complex. They will care for you," I urged. But she could not be convinced. She felt what I was telling her could not happen to us. But it did!

That evening I went to visit the leader of the Hindu religion in our village. While speaking with him regarding our salvation in Jesus, I heard the distant sound of hundreds of people yelling and the roaring of numerous motor vehicles on the road coming into our village. I learned later that 27 cars and trucks and more than 200 motorcycles had arrived loaded with angry men all armed with sharp weapons.

I ran toward our house with the angry shouts of "God is Great. Long live the purity of the Islam religion! Karlos must go!" following behind me. Because they had taken over our village, and were closing in on our house to find and kill me, after ordering my wife to run for her life I leapt out a window and ran hiding in the tapioca field behind our house.

When I ran I felt the beams of their flashlights sweep across me and the tapioca field where I was hiding, but it seems God had temporarily blinded them. They did not or could not see me. But I wept for my wife and child. I knew they were after me; I hoped they would spare my family.

Burned Out!

From my hiding place, I heard the explosions of the small incendiary bombs and, because they had sprinkled gas on the church, I saw the flames ignite and soar upward. I knew our church and house was going up in flames with the good possibility that my wife and child would be burned to death in those flames.

But our God intervened. As I leapt out the window and ran into the nearby tapioca field, my wife scooped up our four-year-old daughter from her bed and, though seven months pregnant with our second child, ran out the back-door where she nearly fainted falling into the hands of the masses looking for me.

In that moment God gave her supernatural strength to rise and run—right through the masses—to a Muslim neighbor's house a short distance away where she was pulled inside and hidden in their bedroom. And amazing! No one saw her and our daughter made no sound during this run! God had tightly closed her lips so she could not even cry.

In the midst of this confusion were two policemen: one a Christian, and the other a Muslim. While the church was burning, the Muslim policeman, angry at what he saw going on and the lack of human compassion and undisciplined emotion of those of his own religion, drained some gas from his own motorcycle with intent to sprinkle and burn some of the vehicles in which the masses had arrived.

After looking through his pockets, he realized he had no matches. So he went and asked his buddy, the

Christian policeman, for a match. "What for?" was the question his buddy asked. And the Muslim policeman answered, "I've had enough! This is not right. I do not agree with what is happening, and I'm out to burn up a few of their vehicles!"

But his Christian buddy answered, "Don't! Our religion teaches us to love. Maybe Karlos is still alive. If we do that, they will never be satisfied until they find and kill him. Our religion tells us that if a man throws stones at you, you are to answer by giving him a banana!" And the Muslim policeman hung his head and fell silent.

At the crack of dawn the next morning, the Muslim family where my wife, Suarti, was kept in hiding, took her and our daughter to the home of one of our church members, Mr. Eddy. At that precise time, I was cautiously making my way to his house from where I had been hiding in the tapioca field. I knocked at Eddy's door, and when he opened it I was shocked to see my wife and child standing there behind him. Seeing me, my wife burst into tears for she thought for certain I had been killed. However, because of our Heavenly Father, my family was still alive.

Throughout that night, and for several days afterward, the leader split the masses into smaller groups, assigning them specific areas of our community to search for me. Even while hiding in the house of Mr. Eddy, one of the Muslim school children came asking for me. Seeing me he said, "We have been ordered to search until we find you. You had best get out of this village." I knew his purpose was to find me and report back to the leader of the masses for them to come and take my life.

Hearing what had happened, and fearing for my life, one of my friends requested a member of the local military to come to Karang Sari with all haste to look for me and to take me and my family out of the area and away from the masses still seeking my life. About 10 o'clock that morning they arrived at Mr. Eddy's house. The military officer immediately pressed us to get into his vehicle. He sat us in the middle between the driver and himself next to the passenger door. My friend, Mr. Naingolan, sat guarding the back door of the vehicle.

"There are many people still out on the road looking for you," the military officer said to me. "If they recognize you when we drive through them and try to stone our vehicle, don't panic. Only if I am killed with this pistol in my hand will they be able to harm you. You have my promise of protection."

And amazing! We drove without incident through those large groups of people congregated along the side of the road looking for me. Some saw the car, and even though others looked inside, they did not see us. God was protecting us. Arriving at the police post, the military officer angrily castigated the police force because of their inability to maintain the peace of the area.

Eventually we were taken to our own church office in Bandar Lampung where we stayed about a month and a half. Then, by invitation, we went to the home of Mr.

Yonas, our friend from Menado. It was there that we awaited the birth of our second child, who was born two weeks later. This child was given the name Stephanus for, as Mr. Yonas said, "He was born in adversity."

Chapter 24

That "Crazy Evangelist!"

Because those of this other religion in three Government districts were hunting for us, it was felt the point of wisdom to move us back to Jakarta for a time. Once there the leadership of our church, the Evangelical Church of Indonesia, asked us to pastor one of our churches without leadership at that time. Though we wept at having to leave the congregation at Karang Sari, we too felt it best to leave the area, at least temporarily.

We were asked to take over the pastoral care of our church in Cileduk and served there for a year and a half. Following that, we were asked to give pastoral leadership to the GIDI church in Jati Asih in the Bekasi area. God greatly blessed that ministry with increasing numbers, and many souls came to know Christ.

Many of the members of this church at one time were rough brutal men—given to violence, robbers, pickpockets, drunkards—all who have been gloriously saved and whose lives have been transformed because of the

Word of God which we taught them. The church numbers increased with many new faces, those who made a commitment to Jesus Christ and joined in our worship times. We served that pastorate for ten years and were greatly encouraged at the numbers and spiritual maturity of those in that congregation. But I could not forget my friends in Lampung.

I had a strange stirring in my heart that our work there was not finished and I began to pray, "Lord, is it your will for me to continue to pastor your congregation here in this suburb of Jakarta? I know that I am an evangelist; I cannot forget the villages in Lampung which are yet unreached with the Gospel. Is this your will for me and is it your time for me to return to search for souls in those villages?"

After praying this for several days, I had a strange stirring in my heart to meet with a member of the Police Department of the Southern District of Lampung whom I had previously met. While still at Karang Sari, I was given the opportunity to lead both him and his wife to the Lord after which they had burned their fetishes. For several days, I felt this urge and the more I prayed about it, the stronger it became. So I said to my wife one day, "Dear, it seems that I must leave for Lampung."

"Leave for Lampung," she wailed. "Look! Your kids need money for school. The rice bin is empty. What do you think your family will eat in your absence? Think! Our Scriptures tell us that you are to begin at Jerusalem and that means your family first!" And I had to confess she was right! But when I went into our bedroom to pray, the urge that I must leave for Lampung increased in intensity.

So I said again to my wife, "I must go. I will use the 20,000 rupiahs (US$2) I have in my pocket to go to the terminal in Pondok Gede where I can check the ATM to see if there are any funds available in our account. If the origin of this urge in my heart is from God, there will be funds and I will leave for Lampung. It is certain that the Lord will send someone to bring food for our table," and I left for the terminal, using the Rp. 20,000 I still had in my pocket.

Arriving at the bus terminal, I began to walk around in the terminal praying and humming to myself the words of the chorus, *"Bersama dengan Allah ku lakukan perkara yang besar,"* meaning, "When one with God, I can do the impossible." Then, I would check our account at the ATM to see if any funds had been given. But there were none except the Rp. 50,000 (US$5) balance. So I would walk about again singing my song and praying: then go and check. Again nothing!

The third time as I was walking about singing, I had to cross the main busy street, and while doing so, a taxi pulled up beside me and stopped. "Hey, friend Karlos," he said, "where do you want to go?" Surprised, I looked up to see a man whom I had led to the Lord a few weeks before; he had made a profession to receive Christ as his Savior. "I'm looking to go to Lampung," I answered.

"Well, come on; get in," he said. "I'll take you to the bus terminal." "Thank you," I said, but did not make an attempt to get in. "Come on, get in," he said. Again I said, "Thanks, my friend, but you just go on. I'll probably just go back home from here." "Karlos," he firmly said, "If you won't get into my taxi and let me help you to the terminal, I'm not going anywhere."

So I went over to where he had stopped his taxi and said to him, "Friend, I apologize to you. It is not that I reject your ride; it is that I am penniless and that meter keeps reminding me of what I need to be paying you for your help." "Oh," he said. "Forget the meter, I can handle that. Just get in and I'll take you to the terminal at Kampung Rambutan." That was several miles away.

So he did, and when we got there he handed me another Rp. 20,000. With that, I climbed on a bus and headed for the ferry at Merak at the end of the island. I needed to get on a ferry there to cross the strait between the island of Java and Sumatera, then another bus ride to Lampung.

As we were nearing Merak, my cell phone rang. It was my wife. "Karlos, Karlos," she said excitedly. "Come home. Come home quick. I've got money for your trip."

"From whom did that come?" I asked. "The nephew of your friend, the policeman, came by and gave us a million rupiahs (US$100)," she exclaimed and begged me to hurry back home to get it.

That "Crazy Evangelist!"

"Praise the Lord," I said, "but I'm already on the toll road to Merak. I can't turn around and come home." I heard her laugh into the phone as she said, "You crazy evangelist. Where did you get the money to get on that bus?"

A short time later she called again, urging me to return home because a friend from Papua had come by wanting to speak with me. What should I do? In that bus I bowed my head and prayed, "Lord, what do you want me to do? Should I go back because of my family, or should I continue on with my trip?" I felt His quiet whisper saying, "Go on. I have work for you in Lampung."

Arriving at the ferry dock in Merak at the western end of the island of Java, I had the grand sum of Rp. 5,000 (fifty cents) left in my pocket and I was only a third of the way to Lampung, my destination. With that few cents, I went to purchase a ticket on the ferry which would take me across to the southern tip of the island of Sumatera and from where I would somehow, someway—God's way—take a bus to the city of Bandar Lampung, two hours away.

Before I could purchase that ticket, a man whom I did not know approached me and invited me to eat with him. "Thank you, Sir," I said, but did not respond. I was truly hungry but I remembered that all I had in my pocket was enough to get me across to the bus terminal on the other side of the strait.

"Come on," he urged. "Have something to eat with me. Don't worry, I'll pay for it." So I did help myself to some food and sat down beside him to eat and chat.

I don't know why, but I suddenly had the urge to share with him the story of the prodigal son from Luke chapter 15. I did not know that I was speaking with the captain of the ferry. After I explained the story, he looked at me and asked, "Friend, I don't want to be disrespectful but where are you going?" And I replied, "I'm on my way to Bandar Lampung."

He then asked, "Have you purchased your ticket yet,?" to which I had to honestly reply, "Not yet." "Okay," he said, "Come with me," and he invited me to the ship. I was a bit anxious thinking, "Hopefully he is not planning any harm to me," but because he pressed me, taking my hand and gently pulling me toward the ship, I went with him.

After getting onto the ship, I thought he would leave me in the large room where the passengers waited on their way across the strait, but he led me right to the bridge, his work place, "You wait here," he said. "I have to go out and organize the ship's crew so we can leave the harbor, but I will be back and we can talk more here." Since now he was wearing the clothes of a captain, I was shocked when I realized that all this time I had been speaking to the captain of the ship.

After he had worked his ship out of the harbor, he returned to his place on the bridge where I was still waiting for him, and locked the door. Uninterrupted, he wanted

That "Crazy Evangelist!"

to hear more of the story of the prodigal son, which I was happy to share with him. As I spoke, I noticed tears forming in his eyes.

When I finished he turned toward me and said, "Friend. Do you know my situation? That son who went astray... I am he! I am a man from Toraja, a Christian province. I'm from a Christian family. I went to Sunday School; I went to church; I read my Bible; I memorized Scripture. But because I went to work with the people on the island of Banten who are Muslims, I renounced Christianity, became a Muslim and married according to the Muslim faith. Please, oh please, pray for me. I want to come back to God."

I prayed with him and led him to make a decision to receive Christ as his Lord and Savior. And he was born anew becoming a member of the Kingdom of God.

Arriving on the other side of the strait, I exited the ferry and made my way to the small bus terminal, hoping to befriend a bus driver who was of the Batak tribe, and normally at least a nominal Christian. On the way to the terminal, a Batak policeman saw me and shouted, "Hey, friend. Where are you wanting to go?" I replied, "I'm on the way to the house of my police friend, Mr. Sinaga."

"Something you need to see him about?" he asked. "Yes," I answered. "I have a strong stirring in my heart to meet with him." His next comment surprised me, "Please don't get on that bus yet. Let's have a cup of coffee first; I need to speak with you."

As we drank our coffee, he poured out his heart regarding a personal problem he had with his superior and asked me to pray with him. After praying, as I turned to continue my journey he stuck something in my pocket saying, "Friend. This is for a cold drink somewhere along your way."

I sat in the front of the bus next to the driver. After settling into my seat, I remembered that my friend, the Batak policeman, had stuffed something into my shirt pocket. I pulled it out. Surprised, I saw that it was a Rp. 50,000 bill (US$5) which he had given me—and I thanked the Lord for this provision for my trip.

Since I had taken a seat next to the driver who was also a Batak, I took the opportunity to witness to him in his own language for I was becoming fairly fluent in it. When the assistant to the driver came by to collect my fare, the driver told him not to ask for money from the black man from Papua. I tried several times to pay, but was refused. He did not want to take my money. Arriving at the Raja Basah terminal in Bandar Lampung, I still had the Rp. 50,000 given to me by the policeman and the remaining Rp. 5,000 from the money I brought from Jakarta.

I continued my way to the home of Mr. Sinaga, my friend in the police department. I learned later that at the precise time I was burdened to go to Bandar Lampung, Mr. Sinaga was also searching for my address and phone number to contact me to come to Bandar Lampung to visit a man he had put in jail because of some crooked business dealings. He had said to his wife that it was important for Karlos to come to minister to this man in jail that very evening.

At the very moment I arrived at his house, his wife was looking for my address and telephone number. When she looked out the window and saw me in front of their house, she called out to her husband, "Dear, look! Who is that standing out in front of our door?" Mr. Sinaga turned to look out the front window. Seeing me, he opened wide the door, exclaiming, "Thank you, Lord. This is a great blessing and an answer to our prayers for we were just looking for your address and telephone number to ask you to come."

When he said, "This is a great blessing," I thought he had been given some money and was going to share it with me, at least to give me funds to return to Jakarta, but I was mistaken. His motivation went beyond the material; it was embedded in the eternal. His purpose in trying to contact me was because of a man he had put in jail who needed to hear the Gospel, and I was called to share that News with him.

When this man in jail saw me, he immediately said, "Help me. Please help me get out of this place," for he thought I was a policeman who came to get his release.

"My friend," I said. "The laws of the land must run their course. I have nothing to do with them. But I want to tell you that there is a freedom far greater than freeing you from this jail. The freedom of which I speak is found in Someone whom you do not know, and that is Jesus Christ. He alone is able to free your soul in a spiritual sense giving you a peace in your heart you have never known; He will also give the police the discernment to know how best to help you." "That is what I want," was his reply.

Hearing his reply, Mr. Sinaga, my police friend, immediately ushered him out of the cell and into his home behind the jail to be able to speak more privately. Once there I shared more in depth about Jesus, the Prince of Peace, and the salvation He has provided for those who have sinned. "My friend," I said. "You have sinned and need to repent and receive Christ as your Savior." It seems those words touched something deep within him, for he began weeping again, asking for Mr. Sinaga to help free him.

Mr. Sinaga answered him, saying, "Don't speak to me about your physical freedom. Listen to what Karlos is telling you and receive the gift of spiritual freedom found only in Jesus Christ." He finally understood and said, "I want to receive Him," and he did as we prayed together.

After we had prayed, Mr. Thomas, the man who had asked for him to be arrested because of a debt incurred, came unannounced into the house of my police friend, Mr. Sinaga. Surprised and irritated that his debtor was out of the cell, sitting there in the house, Mr Thomas said to Mr. Sinaga of the Police Department, "Why is this man not sitting in his cell? Why have you given him his freedom? His debt with me has not yet been settled!"

That "Crazy Evangelist!"

With a smile on his face, Mr. Sinaga, a genuine believer, turned to him and said, "My friend, come sit down inside and hear what has just taken place." He then introduced me to Mr. Thomas and we shared with him the story of Jesus who came to forgive us and to free us from the cell of sin. Hearing what had happened, the heart of Mr. Thomas was touched and he said, "Don't just pray for him; I, too, need your prayers." And I prayed for them both.

Then another incredible thing happened. Mr. Thomas turned to my police friend, Mr. Sinaga, asking that his debtor be released, which he did. Though his debt to Mr. Thomas was in the millions of rupiahs (hundreds of dollars) he forgave him, not demanding that money be repaid. The details of the problem I was not told, but I did work with this family explaining more in detail the salvation experience, then spent several weeks discipling them in the faith. It was precious to be a part of the transformation which took place in their lives.

Chapter 25

A Jihadist Becomes a Pastor

There is a suburb of the city of Bandar Lampung where reside many from those of the Hindu faith. One day I went with my friend Mr. Kimsang to visit his older brother, Mr. Kimnyut, in this suburb and had the opportunity to witness to him of salvation in Christ Jesus.

After I went home that afternoon, in the middle of the night Mr. Kimnyut, who had until then refused to make a decision for Christ, turned off all the lights in the house and said, "If Jesus is indeed the Son of God and my Savior, I ask for two convincing signs: First, show yourself to me now and I will believe in You. Secondly, within this week, please help me obtain 15 million rupiahs (US$1500) to pay the heavy burden of my debt." And he waited.

Suddenly, the room in which he was sitting lighted up and he saw a cross displayed on the wall before him. So bright was the light that he covered his eyes and fell on his knees. In the end his wife and children repented of their sins and put their faith in Jesus Christ as their Lord and Savior. Two weeks later, God in his grace granted his second request by providing the 15 million rupiahs (US$1500) needed to pay off his debt.

Through these two families, Mr. Kimsang and his older brother, Mr. Kimnyut, many of their friends rejected their Hindu religion and accepted Christ as their Savior. Today, there are more than twenty-five active believers who gather weekly in Mr. Kimsang's home to worship together. Mr. Thomas also joined in worship with this small congregation; he, too, was feeling the joy of his salvation experience.

Several months after the Thomas family received Christ and responded positively to the teaching of the Word, there arose in their hearts the strong desire to reach out to their extended family who had not yet surrendered to Christ. Together we made Mr. Thomas' extended family our prayer and witness focus, as well as other ethnic groups in that area, to bring them to Christ.

This effort of evangelism brought many who had not known Christ to believe in Him. Since this group grew rapidly in numbers and in maturity, we gave this church-plant in the geographical area called Kimiling to a man called Mr. Sucipto to pastor. Here is his remarkable story:

Mr Sucipto, a rising star in a fanatical Muslim group, was the one who organized the event of the burning of our church in Karang Sari. He was not directly involved but worked through the younger members of his followers. He was the one designated to organize an event with the explicit purpose of taking my life. For this he had been given 75 million rupiahs, (US$7,500). 50 million rupiahs (US$5,000) was for my head and 25 million rupiahs (US$2,500) was given to take the lives of my family and destroy our home and church at Karang Sari. The church was burned down but our lives were spared.

After our church was burned, he had to report back to his Muslim leaders who had placed this bounty on my head that his efforts at disposing of me had failed. Therefore it was up to him to produce another plan to rid the community of me; that plan was to cast a spell or curse on me so that I would die.

I learned later that the same day this curse was placed on me I had an accident with my motorbike running up under the bed of a truck carrying rocks and gravel to a construction site. Fortunately my life was spared, though my helmet was split open where my head hit the back of the truck.

Another time he heard that a team of evangelists was coming from Jakarta to his village. Since disposing of me had twice failed, and since the bounty on my head had already been paid to him, he was obligated to either dispose of me or replace my death with the death of another pastor-evangelist. So he, with several members of his group, went to raise havoc in the revival services to be held.

A Jihadist Becomes a Pastor

As the preacher began his message that evening, Mr. Sucipto stepped closer to the church and from outside the building threw his powerful magical spell/curse toward the speaker on the platform, burning out the sound system. Aware of the power of darkness about him, the speaker shouted, "Hallelujah," and continued preaching.

Hearing that response, and angered that it had not silenced the preacher, Mr. Sucipto bravely stepped into the doorway of the church and again cast his magical spell toward the evangelist. This time that power of evil reversed itself, reflected back and hit him, knocking him unconscious to the ground.

In that state of unconsciousness, he said he was taken to two different worlds. One was a realm of pitch-black darkness with sounds of weeping and wailing emanating from within that darkness. Clearly he could hear the words, "Heeelp me. Heeelp me!"

From there he was taken in his unconscious state to the realm of pure light. These are his own words:

> "The light was far greater than an electric lamp. It was impossible for me to look at it. Fearfully I asked, 'Who are you?' and a soft gentle voice responded, 'I am *Isa*, the One whom you hate. And this is the Kingdom of Peace.'
>
> "The effect was so great that I made a decision not to return to the real world, but the

voice continued. 'You must return. I want you to be a herald sharing my name, *Isa*, with your family and friends. You must return.'"

Indeed he did not want to return, but the Voice from the Light said he had to go back "to tell others about my name." Immediately he woke up, wondering what had happened to him and why he was in the church with people gathered around him singing hymns and wiping the blood and spittle from his mouth.

Turning to the evangelist, Mr. Sucipto asked, "What was the power that struck me?" The pastor replied, "It was the power of Jesus, the One your holy book refers to as '*Isa*.'" Whereupon Mr. Sucipto asked, "Who is this Jesus, and who is *Isa*?"

After being led into a personal relationship with Jesus Christ, Mr. Sucipto renounced his affiliation with the Muslim religion, including his Muslim name, and took the name Sucipto. Shortly thereafter he was baptized and entered Bible School to become a soldier of Jesus Christ.

After graduating from Bible School, he met with me to declare his desire to join me in ministry. It was in this context that we asked him to take the responsibility of pastoring that church in Kimiling. This enabled me to focus on evangelism and discipleship of the members of the new church-plant in Bumi Asri, in the home that was leased by Mr. Thomas. That is where you will find him at the writing of this book.

The response of this church-plant in Bumi Asri has produced a level of joy in me which I had not experienced before because each of the members of this church-plant expresses a deep burden given to him by the Lord to bring new people into the Kingdom.

Through our joint ministry, the home rented by one of our committed members is no longer large enough to accommodate all the new believers coming to us. Most of these are converts of the Buddhist religion, but there are also those from the Muslim and Hindu faiths as well as the Konghucu, a variant of the Buddhist religion.

Since the building will no longer accommodate the numbers, we had been asking the Lord for a permanent building large enough for our needs. It appears that prayer has been answered because the Lord moved the heart of one of our members to obtain a piece of property for that purpose; it was priced far beyond our financial ability.

We will call the name of this place of worship, "Ebenhaezer," meaning "God supplies," because God has graciously supplied the property; He has assisted us in obtaining all the necessary letters of permission from both the government and the community. Also, initial funds to commence building have been given.

To bring the necessary maturity to this church-plant, we have faithfully taught and emphasized the doctrine of salvation for nearly two years, the doctrine of the Holy Spirit for six months, the doctrine of the

Second Coming of Christ for another six months and other important doctrines follow.

It is exciting and very satisfying to hear these new believers verbalize their own convictions concerning these truths. We believe this is the kind of teaching which has brought rapid growth and maturity to this new congregation.

Chapter 26

And the Word Spread: Bukit Kemuning and Beyond

In addition to the new church-plant at Bumi Asri, we also used the opportunities and moved through the doors which opened to us to reach out into other areas. I am aware that as an evangelist God has called me to pioneer the Gospel into villages that did not know Him. When news of our ministry spread out into other areas, groups of interested people sent delegates requesting me to come and minister to them.

On one occasion I was picked up by a man named Huri Wiharto from Bukit Kemuning in the government regional area of Way Kanan where we were given the opportunity to teach the Word. This group under the leadership of Mr. Wiharto has grown both in numbers and in maturity and they are now meeting weekly in their own modest but permanent building with funds supplied by a believer in the Lampung area.

The believers in Bukit Kemuning have become God's divine channel of evangelism into several other villages in the Mesuji area, especially through family connections. These have come requesting our assistance to open new Bible Study groups in their areas.

And the Word spread. . . . . .to Sinar Laga.

After preaching and challenging those who came to a service in a village called Sinar Laga, in the Mesuji area, a man of the Hindu faith came up afterward and with tears in his eyes, said, "Mr. Karlos, I have listened to your message and the teaching of Scripture you have given on the assurance of salvation which one can enjoy in Jesus Christ.

"As of today, I have made a decision to follow Him. There is a plot of ground in front of my house which I had set aside to build a place of worship for us of the Hindu faith. Now, since I am a believer in this One who came bringing us salvation, I want to use it to build our church. Please send us a man who can nurture and instruct us in our newfound faith."

While this group in the Sinar Laga village was praying for this need, God laid it upon the heart of one of His servants to give ten million rupiahs (US$1000) to build a simple wood chapel on the land given by that Hindu convert. Today they are worshipping in that building led by Pastor Sodikin and his family whom we have placed there.

His wife is working with the youth, teaching them to read and write as well as teaching some English. Her husband works as a shoemaker, giving his testimony and spiritually encouraging those who come to have their shoes serviced. This is his entry point and the group is growing. Each evening they move out in a visitation program, sharing their testimony with neighbors around them.

We have been there several times worshipping together in the evenings, and are always amazed at the many from the area who come to join the worshippers in this simple chapel. Because the little building will not accommodate all those who come, we often put up a small tent or tarpaulin outside the chapel to accommodate the numbers.

Both Muslims and those of the Hindu faith come, attracted to our messages on the humanity and the deity of Jesus Christ, because it answers a lot of their questions regarding this Savior. It also makes sense to them when they realize they need such a Savior to provide them with salvation. Our teaching on the assurance of salvation based on the grace and mercy of God seems to meet a special spiritual need with which they struggle.

One time after I had finished speaking and teaching, after all had left a group of about ten men stayed back to speak with us. "Who is this Jesus?" the leader of the group asked. "And why is it that it is not we who are asked to sacrifice to Him, rather it is He who sacrificed for us? This does not make sense!"

A great question, so I turned the question back to him. "If your small child fell into an open well in your yard, would it be possible for that child to save himself, or must you climb down into the well to save him?"

He thought for a moment then said, "It is obvious; I, as his father, would have to climb down into the well and lift him out so he would not die."

I replied, "Dear friend, you are so very right. That is what our heavenly Father did for us. We are that child who fell into the sea of sin. We try to save ourselves through the rituals of our culture and through the formality of our religion, but we cannot. That is why the Holy Spirit and the Living Word came down, penetrating our cultural and religious forms; He became a man like us to lift us out of the sea of sin and to save us. God focused his attention and grace on us who are certainly not worthy of either His attention or His sacrifice for us. How is it possible that we are given His special welcome and attention? But it is true!"

Hearing that, he drew a deep breath and listened carefully as I explained the truth from Scripture. When I finished, he stood up, grabbed my hand and said, "Your illustration makes a lot of sense. It is easy to understand and apply, thank you. When are you coming again? I want to go deeper into this teaching about Jesus." And they left for their homes.

From Sinar Laga we have opened several other bases of evangelism and discipleship with up to twenty-five adults who have opened their hearts to Jesus. If there is funding available, I try to visit these places every two months. When I do, we must borrow chairs from the surrounding homes to provide seating for the many who come.

And the Word spread......to Bilitan.

From there, we were invited by a retired teacher and community leader of the village of Bilitan in South Sumatra to open a Bible Study in his home. His name was Supandi, and this is his story.

After his daughter was introduced to Jesus, she became a devout believer and was ostracized by her family and asked to leave home. She was a very special young lady and loved by her father, who very much felt his loss. One day, at the risk of being killed she went back home seeking reconciliation with her family and especially her father. To her astonishment and in answer to her prayers, her father and family received her back into their home where she carried on a silent witness within the family.

Some time later, this daughter married an evangelist by the name of Martin. Martin was a member of our church, the Evangelical Church of Indonesia in Jati Asih, near Bekasi in the suburbs of Jakarta. This young lady, a devout believer, was attending a Bible School in Jakarta where by chance they met in a bookstore.

Though others had tried to witness to Mr. Supandi without success, during the preparation for the wedding of their daughter to Martin I was able to gain a hearing and share the Gospel with him. He had been a respected teacher in a Muslim school in the Bilitan area and was interested in my explanation regarding the assurance of salvation through Jesus Christ.

After the wedding, the family returned with me to their home in the village of Margotani in the larger area of Bilitan. There the transformation of the Gospel began to take root in his life to the point where he asked me to open a Bible Study in his home.

Two months later he asked his daughter, Martin's new wife, to contact me to open a Bible Study in the village of Totorejo in South Sumatra because his daughter had already shared the Gospel with several families in that area prior to the wedding, and he had observed that these families needed someone to shepherd them.

Hearing that we were going there, he drove the seventy kilometers on his motorcycle to attend the meetings we were having. In one of our services he was deeply touched and saddened that his way of life was not bringing glory to God, and that he was far from God. After the service, with tears in his eyes, he pled with us again to open a Bible Study in his home village of Margotani. The teaching of the Word was deeply affecting him and he wanted more of it.

And the Word spread......to the Komeri tribe.

A month later we were able to begin that Bible Study in the village of Margotani. Being a retired community leader, plus having been a teacher in the Muslim school for years, he was well-known, very influential and well-respected. Having invited his extended family, as well as the many children whom he had taught, that night his home was full of those interested in hearing the Word of God.

When I explained the truth of Scripture regarding the Christian's assurance of salvation, in the middle of my message he stood to his feet wailing, "I've been wrong. Oh, I've been so wrong. Why is it only now that I am learning about this Jesus? I've built many mosques; I've influenced hundreds of children to attend the Muslim school where I taught—the teaching with no clear direction and no clear purpose for the soul. Can God forgive me? 'God, please forgive me.' Beginning this day, I, Mr Supandi, am changing my name to Paul. The rest of my life I want to use serving this Jesus."

To this day, he is the main witness to the Gospel throughout that area. The church-plant in his house continues to grow both in numbers and in maturity as they faithfully meet each week. They are praying for funds to build a small but permanent building in which to worship.

When I have the opportunity to go there, we discuss the Scriptures for hours. They come from all over. When finished with one family, wanting to change my position I begin to move around a bit, but another family comes. When I want to leave, always there is someone who says, "Can you wait just a moment, another family is coming to see you!"

When finally I am able to leave, they phone asking, "When are you coming again? It has already been a month that you have not visited us!" And this was a place that at one time hated the Christians and their Jesus! God has done a miracle of grace in that village.

Mr. Supandi's son-in-law and daughter minister contextually together in the small village of Kali Dua, about twelve kilometers away from her parents. There she has opened a Kindergarten for the children of the area not only to raise their level of education, but to build a bridge to the parents, enabling her to share Christ with them. Her husband, in an effort to identify with and endear himself to that Komeri tribe—another unreached people group—has formed a small co-op to assist them in their economic needs.

Intentionally, he continues low profile, not attending all the worship services. No one knows he is a lay evangelist though in the evenings he gathers with a group in his father-in-law's home to share the Word of God with those who come. He also leads Sunday worship if there is no student or guest speaker from the school. At this date, there are about twenty-five adults meeting in Mr. Supandi's home, ostensibly led by his wife, the daughter of Mr. Supandi whose influence and community respect protect this family in their witness.

And the Word spread......to Batumarta and Margotani.

After we had taught and discussed the Scriptures for three days, because of a wedding in which he had to participate, Mr. Supandi took us in a car to another village called Batumarta, about three hours away. During that visit we were invited to meet an evangelist (lay preacher) by the name of Moses Sawae, who was ministering among a group of transmigrants about an hour's drive from Batumarta. Months before, Moses had contacted Mr. Supandi, inviting us to contact him. Upon our arrival we were very warmly received by both him and his wife.

That evening we met with seven families who were waiting for us to share the Scriptures with them. They also welcomed us with joy, requesting us to assist them in providing a teacher/evangelist for their spiritual needs. Due to the high level of need but limited number of men to pastor these areas, we ended up asking Moses to locate at Margotani, and to take the responsibility of shepherding the church-plant there. Because of his continued burden for those in the transmigrant area, each week he would ride his bicycle several hours each way to keep in touch with that group.

This was real ministry in the field and through those contacts and family connections, the Word spread!

Chapter 27

And the Word Continued to Spread

Mr. Sunyoto

Mr. Sunyoto was formerly a very fanatic Muslim who hated Christians and he was not bashful in letting this be known. He repeatedly argued, "Why do Christians worship a cross which is nothing but a piece of firewood? This is idolatry, which I very much hate." Spitting in contempt, he continued, "In my opinion, I would like to take my bush knife and rid our world of all Christians, because they are infidels."

Mr. Sunyoto owned a Muslim school and, because he built the school, felt that the door of heaven was always open to him, and that he would be welcomed there.

After becoming a believer through observing the Christian's way of life and testimony, he went to the city looking for work and again observed that the Christians were different from those of the Muslim faith. Attracted to their way of life, he tried various churches in hopes there would be one where he was accepted, but they all feared him because of his prior hatred of the Christians.

Finally, he took a course in evangelism being given by one of the churches in Bandar Lampung and was so moved by the emphasis on evangelism taught in that course that, upon finishing, he became a devout believer. In searching for a church having the same emphasis, he met a man from our Bumi Asri congregation who brought him to my house to introduce him to me.

They knocked on my door, which I opened and politely invited them in. After some small talk, I said to Mr. Sunyoto, "Friend, from whom did you hear about me that you wanted to find me here?" And he replied, "I heard your name from my friend, Mr. Hartoyo, with whom you shared the Gospel several months ago."

Mr Hartoyo was one of several leading Muslim men promoting Islamic law in Lampung who had become a believer before this incident. I had discussed the salvation message and experience with him several times without a definite decision from him. But attracted to the Gospel message, on his own he had secretly purchased a Bible. For six months he had studied its message, after which he committed himself to the Lord and became a believer. It was Mr. Hartoyo who sent him to me.

As we sat chatting that evening, Mr Sunyoto saw on the wall of my home next to a calendar the letters "GIDI," and asked the meaning. "GIDI is the abbreviation for the name of our church," I answered, "which is, Gereja

Injili Di Indonesia." (This translated is, "The Evangelical Church of Indonesia.) and I continued, "The name of our church is meant to emphasize the ministry of evangelism as found in the book of Acts chapter 1 verse 8 which reads:

> "...you will receive power when the Holy Spirit comes on you and you will be my witnesses in Jerusalem, and in all Judea and Samaria, and to the ends of the earth."

His response was immediate. "If that is the emphasis," he asked, "is there any problem with me joining with GIDI? At this very point in time, I am desperately looking for a church which takes seriously the ministry of evangelism."

I responded, "The door of GIDI is open to you. We do not want to pull you away from your own church. We do want you to be active in bringing people to Jesus Christ." He went home, inviting his wife to join him in becoming regular members of our church, which they did. Today both are very active in the effort of evangelism within our church.

To Candipuro and Tritunggal

Several months after Mr. Sunyoto joined our church, together we went to the villages of Candipuro and Tritunggal. We went from house to house introducing Jesus as the Savior of the world, and praying for the sick, the lame, the blind, and the deaf.

As we entered one of the homes we realized that we were being seen as those with psychic or supernatural power, so I immediately said to them, "Friends, we who have come are neither shaman manipulating the power of the spirits through ritual, nor medical doctors using medicine. We bring only the name of the One who has authority over heaven and earth. This name has made the lame to walk, the blind to see, and the deaf to hear," and I began to teach them about Jesus as found in both our Bible and their holy book, the *Qur'an*.

All were enthusiastically listening and paying attention to the explanations I was giving when one of the older men stood to his feet, asking, "Why are Christians asked to worship three gods, and how is it possible for God to have a son as you Christians believe?" Those two questions trouble every devout Muslim.

To answer his question, I took an orange from the table and said, "Look. This is one orange in my hand. This orange has a skin, it has fruit on the inside which we enjoy eating, and inside that fruit we find seeds. Does this mean that I have three oranges?" "No!" they answered in unison.

I gave another illustration. "Think with me about fire," I said. "There is the flame of fire; there is the warmth of that fire, and there is the light of that fire. Does that mean there are three different fires?" I asked. Again, they shouted, "No! There is only one fire."

"Let me give you one more illustration," I said. "What about the sun? There is the sun; there is the light of that sun; and there is the warmth of that sun. Does that mean there are three different suns?" I asked. Again their response was, "There is only one sun."

I went on to explain that we do not worship three gods; we worship only one. "Your *Al-Qur'an* says, *'Whosoever worships three gods is an infidel.'* Our Bible also says in the book of Exodus chapter 20, *'Thou shalt have no other gods before me.'*

Please allow me to ask you why you have in your house sacred fetishes which you respect and worship?"

They were all silent then one of them said, "We don't have any." And I replied, "This man whom you have placed in front of me to be healed has become lame because of the *kris*, which you have in that room behind him." (The *kris* is a special long sword type of instrument having special spirit power to protect the family.)

I continued, "In the drawers of that cupboard you have hidden some of your fetishes and before the threshold of your home here you have buried a spirit idol over which you have recited your spirit incantations to protect your home." All fell silent in fear; they knew I was speaking the truth.

After a moment of silence, I asked, "What do you want to do? Do you want to sacrifice this lame man or do you want to sacrifice your sacred fetishes?"

Their response was, "Please, not this man; we will sacrifice our household gods." To which I replied, "If that is your desire, bring your fetishes and household gods and we will burn them in the name of Jesus."

This they did and when we prayed in the name of Jesus, while those gods were still burning, the lame man began to move his legs and was able to lift his feet. When with help from his family he sat up, those in the room realized something very special had happened and great was the effect on all who witnessed it.

So I said to the group that had gathered, "The Lord Jesus is present in this home and wants to heal this man. Do you believe that Jesus is God and your Savior who can heal this man?" This was after I had explained salvation found only in Christ. Some were silent; others said, "Yes, hopefully it is the will of God." "Hopefully?" I replied, "No, not hopefully, but certainly. You must believe that He is God and that He wants to heal this lame man."

An older man stood to speak. "My friends of the Muslim faith," he began, and I thought he was probably going to rebuke me but he went on to say, "All these years we have been deluded by teachers of our faith but what this black man says is truth," and all joined in by saying in unison "Aaaamin! Aaaamin!" affirming the teaching I had given.

The following week, we visited an older lady who had been blind for six years. We explained the Scriptures as we had the week before, and confronted those who had gathered regarding the sacred spirit objects kept in the house. When they brought these to me, I again asked, "Do you want to sacrifice these fetishes, or do you want to sacrifice the eyesight of this your mother?"

This lady, along with her children, replied, "We will sacrifice the fetishes. Of primary importance is the sight of our mother." Then we urged them to receive Jesus Christ as their Savior. After both Mr. Sunyoto with his wife had prayed, I too, led in prayer.

Following prayer, the mother said, "Oh, I'm seeing just a little light," and I ran and stood before the door, holding up both my hands, "My mother," I said, "… look toward the door. What do you see?" And she said, "I see something like a block of wood standing in the doorway." So we prayed again.

After praying, I went again to the doorway and held up my hand. "My mother, look again toward my hand. How many fingers am I holding up?" She looked intently for a moment and said, "I see five fingers." I held up three fingers asking, "How many do you see now?" She responded immediately, "Three." Finally, I held up only one finger and she said, "One," and with that the entire family, who had witnessed this, broke out weeping. Today she is working in the rice paddies along with the other women. God has healed her!

The next week, while ministering in like manner to several deaf people, we saw the Lord bring hearing and soul healing to them. He was obviously at work in this community, giving evidence of His existence and the power in His Word of Truth.

Chapter 28

Christmas....in the Citra Village

News of these healings spread throughout the community. We were nearing Christmas at that time, and had prepared chairs for 300 people in a large public building where we were to have our Christmas program. To our utter amazement, there were nearly 400 people—far more than the number of chairs we had provided—who came to hear the message I had prepared on the theme, Jesus Christ, the Savior of the World.

Three hours before the program began, members of the Marine Corps as well as the police arrived to provide security and to guarantee that our celebration would proceed as planned without disruption, physical confrontation, or even throwing of rocks, from the fanaticism of the other local religions.

These security forces were in place and our service was already in process when four buses and dozens of motorcycles arrived to join in our celebration and worship service. In spite of the added numbers, the service continued with orderliness, calmness, and necessary restraint. Many voiced the blessing the Christmas service had been to them and, following the service, many came inviting us—even begging us—to come and minister to them in their homes.

This ministry I surrendered to Mr. Sunyoto for him to be responsible for its continuation. We began our worship services in his home and had been meeting there for a couple of years, when suddenly one Sunday we were surrounded by a group of jihad soldiers, all wearing their white hats. They ordered us outside to be questioned.

Because I was the guest of Mr. Sunyoto, I did not have the right to speak. He did the talking. If I had spoken, they could immediately say, "Why is this black man from Papua doing the talking? This proves he has come to make Christians out of these people in our community." So I kept quiet; Mr. Sunyoto replied to their questions.

Unknown to us, while he was speaking to them, his wife slipped inside and called for the Marine Corps. They came immediately, but by the time they arrived, the masses had dispersed and the leaders had gone into hiding. Still, these Marines spoke with the local government personnel, informing them that they were required to maintain peace. They would be monitored to make sure they did not run from that responsibility.

Because of the situation, for security reasons, we felt it wise to not continue meeting for worship in large groups. So we split into smaller cells going from house to house teaching the lessons of Scripture.

In this manner, through lessons which I prepare for Mr. Sunyoto, we are still ministering to this congregation of about twenty-five adults who meet for worship on Sunday and Thursday. I quietly slip into the group about once a month, visiting and praying with these families. To be seen there more often would put the group at risk. I must be careful for I am being followed.

Though invitations via phone calls continue to come, the color of my skin makes me immediately high profile and raises suspicion as to my reason for being in the community. Thus I have put limitations on myself to not be a hindrance to the spread of the Gospel throughout that community.

Chapter 29

Experiencing "God Things" in Ministry

Provision for my Family

One time I was totally without funds for several days. I had no gas for my motorcycle; I had no food for our table. Meanwhile, my wife phoned me to remind me that our first child, Irma, had to register to enroll in High School, and needed money. What should I do? What could I do?

That evening I went to bed with this need on my mind. About 4 o'clock in the morning I was awakened by Someone in a white robe who came and touched my feet. Opening my eyes, I saw this One in white standing near my feet, and He said, "I've come to tell you that there are funds in your bank account." I wiped my eyes to see if this was real, and when I looked again he was gone.

About 6 o'clock that next morning I went to the ATM to find that indeed someone had placed five million rupiahs (US$500) in our account. When the bank opened at 8 o'clock that morning, I was there asking that the numbers be printed in my bank book. The figure was printed but with no indication of its origin, so I asked the bank teller who might have sent it. She checked further then said, "Yes, there is evidence that it was credited to your account, but no indication as to who sent it. Maybe it was from another bank." To this day, we do not know from where those funds came. All we know is that in our time of desperate need, God sent someone to meet that need. Irma, my lovely teenager, enrolled in her High School. Thank you Lord.

The testimony of the leader of the NU who believed

One day Mr. Thomas contacted me to go with him to pray for the leader of a Muslim group called the NU. This man was also a *paranormal*, a psychic, involved with the supernatural...very influential and creepy! Whenever someone was coming to his house he could know beforehand who was coming and that person's purpose.

It seems that this man experienced a problem in his business, and Mr. Thomas contacted me to go with him to pray for him. Arriving at his home, we were invited in and he immediately asked that the God of the Christians help him in his business efforts.

When he said that I turned to him, saying, "My friend, the one causing your business to fail is in your possession; you yourself are the protector of it." Surprised, he said, "What am I protecting that is causing my business to fail?"

I pointed to his bedroom and said, "Forgive me, my friend. We have just met and I do not wish to offend. But I have a feeling that in the corner of your bedroom right behind you is a cabinet, is there not?"

"Yes," he said, "...there is." I continued, "And on the top shelf of that cabinet is the form of a man with long hair. Who is that?" I asked. He was shocked and silent.

I continued. "On each of the shoulders of that image you have implanted a small needle, the symbol of the spirit, to ward off anyone wanting to harm you. Embedded in those lips is something you have placed so that when you speak the spirit will move others to listen and bow to your desires. On its forehead is a symbol of the spirit that subjugates your enemies to you.

"As long as you guard the spirits behind these symbols, though you are convinced they help you, in truth they are your enemies bringing about your destruction. If they cannot take your life, they take your treasures and all the profit from your business. There is nothing free when you are controlled by these spirits from the realm of the power of darkness."

Hearing this he was very shocked and thought to himself, "Normally, I am the one who can read another's thoughts with my physic power but here...how is it possible that this black man from Papua has a higher, more sophisticated, power than mine?" I left him to think.

The following week we went again to his house. "The blessing of God will not ask you to sacrifice your life; God will not rob you of your business profits," I explained. "Only the power of darkness does that. *Isa* (Jesus) *Almasih* is the Great High Priest—our Mediator and Provider. We are going to pray in His name but the condition of His assistance in our lives is that we accept His ministry of mediation by accepting Him as our Savior," I said, and gave this illustration.

"It is like this. If your child comes asking for money, since he is your child, you will give it to him. But if I ask you for money, there is no possibility you would give it to me. The same goes for your relationship with *Isa Almasih* (Jesus Christ). If you are yet outside his family, He cannot give to you. So, my friend, the question is, are you ready to receive Him as Lord and Savior of your life and to become by adoption a member of His family?" Though he understood, he was not yet ready for that radical a commitment, so we prayed and I went home.

That evening he sat pondering our visit and began connecting the truths we had left with him, that *Isa Almasih* was indeed the Messiah and that it was thus written in the *Al-Qur'an*. So he telephoned Mr. Thomas asking for that black man from Papua. A short time later, we arrived at his home where he was waiting for us with his family.

We explained again that *Isa Almasih* (Jesus the Messiah) was mentioned in both our Scriptures and the Muslim holy book, the *Al-Qur'an*. He was increasingly attracted to this Jesus as we explained from our Scriptures the salvation we can enjoy in knowing Him as our personal Savior. Though not yet a believer, he began coming to our worship services on Sunday even though his wife continued to have her doubts.

Two months later he had an accident and was taken unconscious to the emergency room in the Baptist hospital in Bandar Lampung. He could neither eat nor drink. His neck had been nearly severed from his body. According to the doctor, he had only minutes to live.

Standing beside his bed, the wife of this injured Muslim man prayed, "Lord Jesus. If it is true that you exist and that you are our Lord and Savior, I ask for a miracle." Then her eyes caught the verses found in Matthew 11:28-30 written in big letters on the wall of the hospital room:

> *"Come unto me all you who are weary*
> *and burdened, and I will give you rest.*
> *Take my yoke upon you and learn from me,*
> *For I am gentle and humble in heart,*
> *And you will find rest for you souls.*
> *For my yoke is easy and my burden is light."*

When she read that verse on the wall, suddenly a strange uncontrollable feeling came over her, causing her to bow her head and to begin weeping. According to the doctor there was no hope for her husband but the reverse happened—even the doctor could not believe it. His neck which was nearly severed in the accident slowly began to heal and his body began to respond to the medicine given him.

Finally convinced that Jesus was indeed the Lord God and their Savior, there in the hospital as we ministered to them, they both received Christ as their Savior and were gloriously transformed by their new faith.

Part 6

A Special Message to My Muslim Friends

An Explanation

An Introduction

In my explanation of Christianity to my Muslim friends, and who *Isa Almasih* (Jesus the Messiah) is, I find it both proper and beneficial to link this explanation to their holy book, the *Al-Qur'an*.

One of the most troublesome truths of our Scriptures for the Muslim is our term, Jesus, the Son of God. This reduces the divine to having had a sexual experience with Mary, the mother of Jesus, who gave birth to Jesus, whom we Christians call the Son of God.

Moving out from this misunderstanding are two fundamental questions the devout Muslim asks:

1. Why do Christians worship three gods?

2. How is it possible for God to have a son? Can God be married, or be given in marriage? Can God have children, or become someone's child? When did God marry so as to have a child called "Jesus, the Son of God?"

An Explanation of Christianity to My Muslim Friends

Allow me to respond with "real life" illustrations to these misconceptions of our Christianity. Because of their relevancy in the context of this chapter, I take the liberty to reiterate several illustrations already used in the text narrative.

One evening as I was teaching, one of the older men stood to his feet asking, "Why are Christians asked to worship three gods, and how is it possible for God to have a son as you Christians believe?" Those two questions trouble every devout Muslim.

To answer his first question, I took an orange from the table and said, "Look. This is one orange in my hand. This orange has a skin, it has fruit on the inside which we enjoy eating, and inside that fruit we find seeds. Does this mean that I have three oranges?" "No!" they answered in unison.

I gave another illustration. "Think with me about fire," I said. "There is the flame of a fire; there is the warmth of that fire; and there is the light of that fire. Does that mean there are three different fires?" I asked. Again, they shouted, "No! There is only one fire."

"Let me give you another illustration," I said. "What about the sun? There is the sun; there is the light of that sun; and there is the warmth of that sun. Does that mean there are three different suns?' Again their response was, "There is only one sun."

An Explanation

"And one final illustration," I said. "I have a body; I have a soul; and I have a spirit. Does that mean that I, Karlos, am three people?" They smiled and answered, "No! You are one person."

So I continued, "The body is the visible, touchable, material part of me; the soul is the immaterial, the rational, emotional part of me allowing me to make contact with, and to understand, the feelings and thoughts of others; and the spirit is the component within me which allows me to fellowship and worship God who is also the Spirit. The Spirit influences the totality of our lives, assisting us to enjoy true worship—worship which is acceptable to God."

And I went on to explain that we do not worship three gods; we worship only One God. "Your *Al-Qur'an* says,

> '*Whosoever worships three gods is an infidel.*'

Our Bible also says in the book of Exodus chapter 20 verses 2-3a:

> '*You shall have no other gods before me...*
> *You shall not bow down to them or worship them,*
> *For I, the LORD your God, am a jealous God...*'

We do not worship three gods; we worship ONE GOD in three persons or three identities."

Upon hearing this explanation, my hearers smiled and said, "We very much agree with your explanation."

Then they asked, "How is it that God, the Almighty, whose might and wisdom far surpasses that of man's thoughts, can be called, 'Father?'"

I answered, "I have what we call 'adopted parents.' Does this mean that they gave birth to me? No! I refer to them as 'my father' and 'my mother' because they have voluntarily taken on the responsibility of caring for me. So it is with God who cares for me giving me life and all manner of material and spiritual blessings. It is He who notices and supplies my needs. Therefore, I can justifiably and linguistically call God 'My Father.'

"The terms 'Father' and 'Son' are used to indicate the unity and intimacy which a believer may enjoy personally with a personal God, not a biological relationship on a human level.

"Because He came from His Father God and, according to John 1:1, because He IS God, Jesus Christ is called 'God's Son' in a special relationship meaning He is the *Logos,* the Word of God, the expression of who God is to us. He is also the Word of Life who was born of the Virgin Mary.

"Finally, the Holy Spirit is also God. It is the Spirit who leads us, walks with us, and makes us aware of sin. The Spirit guides us into all truth found in one source, Jesus Christ, which in the Arab language translated into Indonesian, is *Isa Almasih.*"

Now let me comment to the second question

An Explanation

regarding the term "Son of God."

To answer this question, I normally ask a question of my hearers. "My friends," I ask, "from where do you come?" There are some who answer, "I'm from Java." others respond by saying, "from Cirebon." Still others say, "I'm from Palembang."

And I respond by saying, "If you say, 'I'm from Palembang,' or, 'I'm a child of Palembang,' let me ask you, 'When did the city of Palembang marry and give birth to you?'" Usually all become quiet, unable to answer my question.

So I continue. "If I say, 'I'm from Palembang,' or, 'I'm a child of Palembang,' it simply means that I come from the city of Palembang—a geographical, social connection not a biological one.

"When we say 'school children' we do not mean there is a Mr. 'School Father' and a Mrs. 'School Mother' who gave biological birth to those 'school children.' We understand that such a term means 'those children are going to school.'

"Likewise, the term 'Son of God' means that Jesus comes from God. He originates from God. Because He IS God, God Himself through the Spirit became flesh within the womb of Mary. In other words, the Living Word was transformed into a man within the womb of Mary through an act of the Spirit of God (John 1:1, 14)."

To answer their deeply felt concerns, I continue by explaining that fundamentally, God neither marries, nor can he be given in marriage. He does not have biological children. He has never given birth to a son in a physical sense and He has never been someone's child! [The Christian's terminology confuses this issue.]

Through the work of the Holy Spirit, the Living Word (*Logos*-Jesus*)* of John 1:1 in the womb of Mary was incarnated as a human being so that you, my friends, and I, could know Him. Your holy book, the Qur'ran tells us the same, that *Isa Almasih* (Jesus, the Messiah) is also "The Living Word" (a favorite expression in the *Al-Qur'an*). He was incarnated, that is, transformed in the womb of Mary, and was born a man to reach man and thus to rescue him. This was necessary for our salvation.

The *Al-Qur'an* also tells us that *Isa* (Jesus), the child of Mary, is the greatest and the highest in position both here on earth as well as in heaven. The Holy Spirit produced in Mary's womb this child Jesus, and the power of God, the Almighty, protected Him, stating that He would be called, "the Holy One of *Aoullah* (God)."

An earthly king has authority within his kingdom for as long as he lives. When he dies, the power of his authority dies with him. It is the same with *Isa Almasih*. However, since He has never died, His power and authority continue both here and in heaven; His kingdom has no end, for He lives forever. If *Isa* were only man, his kingdom would long ago have disappeared. But

An Explanation

because He is also God, His government is eternal. It will never end. That, my friends, is the reason the conflict of religions continues.

According to John 1:14, this One born of the Holy Spirit, the Living Word, who became flesh, did not come to bring a religion. He came to bring salvation. There is a wide gulf separating man because of his sin and the Almighty because He is holy. There is only one bridge across this gulf which one must cross to get to God. And that bridge is Jesus Christ.

My dear Muslim friends! The Prophet Muhammad taught his Muslim followers about this bridge. He spoke of this bridge as being *Isa Almasih* (Jesus Christ). One hundred twenty times the name *Isa* (Jesus) is mentioned in the *Al-Qur'an* in ninety-seven different verses of your holy book. Seventy-five percent of those ninety-seven different verses follow the message of our Scriptures.

Isa is our Savior. He did not come to bring a religion. He came to bring salvation. He came to save us from our sins. We are under a curse because of our sins, which will eventually bring upon us the judgment of God. That judgment is eternal separation of God from man. For that reason, God took the initiative and became a True Man for the express purpose of rescuing us and bringing us back to Himself.

Truly, we are unworthy, but because of His love for us, He has provided a way for us to be delivered from our sin and made acceptable to Him. That Way is through *Isa Almasih* (John 14:6).

> *"Jesus answered, 'I am the Way, the Truth and the Life; no one comes to the Father except through Me.'"*

An Invitation:

In closing, I ask you one final question. There are two words consistently and religiously used in your worship of *Aoullah* (God): *sholat*, and *syafaat*. *Sholat* means, "I ask for salvation." *Syafaat* means, "I provide salvation."

My dear friends, you must choose between the two. Do you want to follow the leader who "asks for salvation?" Or do you want to follow and worship the One who "provides your salvation?" Because he is human, the Prophet Muhammad "asks" for salvation; Jesus "provides" it for you. The decision is yours. I cannot force you. I only explain that which is true in the hope that you will choose to follow the One who has provided your salvation through *Isa Almasih*.

I urge you to join many others of your Muslim friends who, upon hearing this Truth, accept Him as their Saviour, clap their hands in affirmation and in unison sincerely respond with, "*Aaaamin*! *Aaaamin*!"